FREUD'S REQUIEM

FREUD'S REQUIEM

Mourning, Memory, and the Invisible
History of a Summer Walk

MATTHEW VON UNWERTH

RIVERHEAD BOOKS
A MEMBER OF PENGUIN GROUP (USA)
NEW YORK
2005

RIVERHEAD BOOKS
Published by the Penguin Group
Penguin Group (USA) Inc., 375 Hudson Street, New York,
New York 10014, USA • Penguin Group (Canada), 90 Eglinton Avenue East, Suite 700,
Toronto, Ontario M4P 2Y3, Canada (a division of Pearson Penguin Canada Inc.)
• Penguin Books Ltd, 80 Strand, London WC2R 0RL, England • Penguin Ireland,
25 St Stephen's Green, Dublin 2, Ireland (a division of Penguin Books Ltd)
• Penguin Group (Australia), 250 Camberwell Road, Camberwell, Victoria 3124,
Australia (a division of Pearson Australia Group Pty Ltd) • Penguin Books India Pvt Ltd,
11 Community Centre, Panchsheel Park, New Delhi–110 017, India • Penguin Group (NZ),
Cnr Airborne and Rosedale Roads, Albany, Auckland 1310, New Zealand (a division of
Pearson New Zealand Ltd) • Penguin Books (South Africa) (Pty) Ltd, 24 Sturdee Avenue,
Rosebank, Johannesburg 2196, South Africa

Penguin Books Ltd, Registered Offices:
80 Strand, London WC2R 0RL, England

Library of Congress Cataloging-in-Publication Data

Unwerth, Matthew von, date.
Freud's requiem : mourning, memory, and the invisible history of a
summer walk / Matthew von Unwerth.
p.   cm.
Includes bibliographical references.
ISBN 1-57322-247-X
1. Freud, Sigmund, 1856–1939.   2. Freud, Sigmund, 1856–1939. Vergänglichkeit.
3. Bereavement—Psychological aspects.   4. Creation (Literary, artistic, etc.).
5. Rilke, Rainer Maria, 1875–1926.   I. Title.
BF109.F74U59   2005   2004065077
150.19'52'092—dc22
[B]

Printed in the United States of America
1   3   5   7   9   10   8   6   4   2

This book is printed on acid-free paper. ∞

Book design by Michelle McMillian

In memory of

K. R. Eissler

and

Alvar Garcia Guerra

Every man sings a requiem to his own heart.

—HIERON, WORKS, 1.432

ACKNOWLEDGMENTS

This book has grown out of my engagement with the idea and the practice of psychoanalysis, and a privileged involvement with the vibrant communities that revolve around them. To the members of those communities, for their conversation, insight, advice, and inspiration, I am gratefully indebted.

I owe specific thanks to the following: Michael Molnar, acting director of the Freud Museum (London); Professor Patrick Mahony and Professor Gerhard Fichtner; David Cashion, for his editorial efforts in the formative stages of this book; Anna Jardine, for her heroic, perceptive, and exhaustive copyediting; at Riverhead Books, Cindy Spiegel, David Moldawer, and especially Jake Morrissey for their patient support, and for seeing it through; Jonathan Galassi, Louis Lauro, Ted Libbey, Dottie Jeffries, and Rick and Sandy von Unwerth; the Goethe-Institut Library (New York); the Thomas J. Watson Library of The Metropolitan Museum of Art; the members and staff of

ACKNOWLEDGMENTS

The New York Psychoanalytic Institute & Society; and Wendy Kraus, for her thoughtful reading, understanding, and love.

Above all, I thank my agent and friend Marly Rusoff, without whose faith, creativity, and tireless effort this work would not have been.

FREUD'S REQUIEM

In the summer of 1913, Sigmund Freud took a stroll in "a smiling countryside in the company of a taciturn friend and of a young but already famous poet." That August he was vacationing in the Dolomites, an epic mountain region at the border of Austria and Italy, amid cinematic, archaic promontories whose profiles resembled dragon teeth. It was a place Freud knew well from his student days in Trieste and from many subsequent holiday rambles. An avid naturalist, who delighted in hunting flowers and mushrooms, he would have reveled in the hardy mountain flora, in the parnassia and primrose, milkwort and rampion, and the fragile hellebore that poke their way each spring through the rocky soil and receding snows.

As Freud and his companions lingered in the soft light of that afternoon, admiring the surrounding nature, their conversation took a melancholy turn. The poet was troubled by ghosts. Everywhere he turned he saw beauty, but in this radiance the poet foresaw the coming of sorrow. All these things were transient, fated to extinction; mocked by its own frailty, beauty was eclipsed by its negation, and had no value and no meaning.

The older man was sympathetic to the poet's melancholy (which their silent friend shared), but he could not accept his anguished conclusion. The poet was correct, of course, that all earthly things must pass away, including those in whose qualities we take special pleasure. But rather than subtract from their beauty, Freud protested, this evanescence only added to beauty's increase. Winter replaces summer, but spring comes again in winter's wake. The scientist—taken aback, perhaps, by the poet's remonstrance—suggested that it was beauty's "scarcity value in time" that gave what is precious its worth. Since beauty was known—could ever be known—only by the heart and eye and mind of its witness, so long as we live, beauty is with us, passing into nothingness only when we, too, cease to exist.

Freud's protests found no favor with the poet, or with their companion, the "taciturn friend." His own conviction, however, remained unshakable, that the fleeting quality of existence increased, not diminished, life's value.

Later, Freud wondered at the source of his companions' attitude that afternoon. Looking back on their conversation, he recognized in them what he called "a revolt in their minds against mourning." They recognized in the transience of these beautiful things the essential mortality of life, and of their own lives; this knowledge so disturbed them that they could no longer appreciate beauty except as something already lost. In the process, life lost for them its luster and meaning.

Freud himself was puzzled by mourning, which he considered love's rebellion against loss. When we love, he said, our love goes out from us to the object of our affection, where it dwells in the beloved as if in ourselves—much like an embassy, which, though in a foreign land, is said to stand upon the soil of the native country. When we lose a loved one, our love is drawn back into us. But this process of recall is arduous and painful. Our love strives to inhabit the dwelling it has built in the heart of our lover, even when that heart no longer beats or is no longer near. And so, losing love, we suffer, and in that suffering we experience our love once more, in parting.

After their conversation, one assumes, the wanderers went their separate ways, each of them confirmed in their own opinion of life's fleeting blessings. We can do no more than assume, though, since here our knowledge of that afternoon ends, and the companions disappear from view with the last mountain light.

What we know of this singular meeting stems from the essay "On Transience," which Freud wrote in 1915, in tribute to the poet Goethe, as World War I raged outside his door at Berggasse 19, in the final days of the glory of the Austro-Hungarian Empire and its most cultivated pearl, the city of Vienna. The poet with whom Freud walked that afternoon has been recognized as Rainer Maria Rilke, and the taciturn friend as Lou Andreas-Salomé, the poet's former lover and eternal muse, and a psychoanalyst and well-known writer.

That Freud withheld the identities of his companions in his essay is perhaps understandable; the piece was published while all three were still living, and Freud always took pains not to draw undue attention to the patients and other subjects who populate his writings. But he went further than that in concealing the people and places that inspired "On Transience."

The afternoon walk, it turns out, may not have been a walk at all, nor can one find in the Dolomites the place where the companions met. Instead, it is known that the poet and the analyst met in a hotel lobby in Munich, during the Fourth International Psycho-analytical Congress in 1913, at which both Freud and Rilke were present, for very different reasons. Freud went to Munich hoping to save his infant science, which was at that moment being seriously threatened by the dissension of his close friend and favorite colleague, Carl Jung. For Rilke, the salvation he sought was his own, as he struggled to rediscover the fugitive source of creative inspiration, upon which he believed his life depended.

The three companions met in Munich—not, in all likelihood, à trois, but in the company of other psychoanalysts attending the Congress, or perhaps with friends of Rilke and Lou. Their intimate conversation might have just as easily been shouted over laughter at a cramped corner table as passed in whispers to circumvent the crowding noise.

What is certain is that the encounter left its mark on the

founder of psychoanalysis, enough for him to revisit it again and again, in an effort to make sense of something that defied his understanding. His disquiet is evident in his attempt to supplement the conversation with second thoughts, his effort to see in it confirmation of his views on mourning, and a reflection of the current affairs of a world gone mad. It is apparent in the essay itself, in the incomparable German that Freud employs to convey the essay's elegant sentiment, which belies the agitation the meeting provoked in him. And it is there also in the work's very conception, in the artful deception of transposing the scene from where it happened to where Freud imagined it.

Around the time he was writing the essay, in late 1915, Rilke saw Freud again, this time at his home. What happened there is shrouded in silence, but Freud later wrote to Lou of the outcome, haunted by the poet's verdict, *"kein ewiger Bund zu flechten,"* that "no lasting bond" could be forged between them. More than this is not known; the two men never met again. In subsequent years, what they knew of each other they gleaned from Lou Andreas-Salomé. This friend remained an enduring, powerful presence in both men's lives, and through her discussions of psychoanalytic ideas with Rilke and her analytic speculations to Freud on the turbulent character of the poet, each of the two men persisted in the mind of the other.

What happened among Freud and Lou and Rilke, and why could no lasting bond be forged between the two men? What made Freud memorialize or possibly invent a summer walk in an essay dedicated to his hero Goethe? These questions are ultimately unanswerable, but are no less compelling for that. For they involve riddles that Freud himself first touched on in his essay on transience, and to which all three protagonists dedicated their lives—mysteries that elude easy comprehension, yet still haunt us.

Behind Freud's brief essay stands a vivid, subterranean realm, joining the three companions to the world of fleeting beauty over which they argued that day, as well as to the real world in which they lived. Regarded from different angles, Freud's sentimental prose poem opens to reveal a panorama of the mind of the man who wrote it, a mind that, for all its generative brilliance, is as sentimental, troubled, and torn as that of any of his patients, or as that of any one of our own. When we peel back its layers, Freud's essay suggests a story of his inspirations and frustrations, his dreams and crises of spirit, a story of his loves and hopes, and above all of his experiences of loss. "On Transience" is a portrait in miniature of the world of its writer, rich and teeming with the same themes that shaped his life and his work.

CHAPTER ONE

In *November,* or perhaps December, of 1915, Freud sat working at his desk, shivering beneath a cloak, his pen trembling. A cold winter was setting in, and Austria was at war, with no end in sight. It was Freud's third war, and the worst he had seen. All but one of his children had left home. His sons Martin and Ernst had been drafted, and for the next several years he would have little news of them, and he frequently feared for their lives. His older daughters, too, now married and living in other cities, were separated from him, prevented from visiting by wartime travel restrictions. Few patients waited outside his consulting room, and the prospect of security that success had only recently brought him seemed again to recede. He was almost sixty, and not far from sixty-one, the age his own superstitious calculations had marked him for death. Now, in his office, in the company of his dogs and his beloved collection of antiquities, Freud was an old man in a world grown suddenly unfamiliar, one that promised nothing new but sorrow.

By war's end, the Europe that Freud had been born into would disappear forever. In the aftermath—with some 16 million deaths, tens of thousands of miles of rails destroyed, and the loss of millions of homes and jobs—were decades of unemployment, inflation, and instability, and ultimately, another war, which would exceed its forebear in brutality.

In the autumn of 1915, Freud was asked to contribute to a special publication, to be called *Das Land Goethes* (Goethe's Land), which was intended to raise money for German libraries. Planned in part as wartime propaganda, the volume was dedicated to Johann Wolfgang von Goethe, the German writer whom Freud admired above all, and aimed to demonstrate the civility of the "barbaric" German nature then vilified by its enemies. Freud was by this time known around the world, and psychoanalysis had become an international movement; yet even for him his fellow contributors to the volume were impressive company: Albert Einstein; the writers Gerhardt Hauptmann, Hugo von Hofmannsthal, Arthur Schnitzler, and Jakob Wassermann; the composers Max Reger and Richard Strauss; and more than a hundred other writers, artists, scientists, politicians, and soldiers. It was to be a lavish production, with expensive reproductions of artworks, manuscripts, and autographs, its large sheets bound in yellow silk.

Freud's feelings about the war were deeply mixed. In the early days of the conflict, he sided patriotically with his nation's army; he wrote his son Martin at the front that he was fighting for a good cause. But in a letter written to Lou Andreas-Salomé in November 1914, Freud sounded a different note. "I have no doubt that humanity will get over this war, but I know for certain that I and my contemporaries will see the world cheerful no more." Ominously, he concluded that "since we can only regard the highest present civilization as burdened with an enormous hypocrisy, it follows that we are organically unfitted for it. We have to abdicate, and the Great Unknown, He or It, lurking behind Fate will someday repeat this experiment with another race. I know that science is only apparently dead, but humanity seems to be really dead." It was an uncharacteristic sentiment, even in jest, for a man whose skepticism firmly opposed any higher power.

His contribution to *Das Land Goethes* was short—just over a thousand words—and filled but a single page. Next to his major works—*Three Essays on the Theory of Sexuality, Papers on Metapsychology, The Ego and the Id, Beyond the Pleasure Principle,* and above all, *The Interpretation of Dreams*—it is a trifle. Yet it is unlike anything he had written before. Though his theme, the origin of mourning, is psychoanalytic, the essay is lyrical, meditative, elegiac—most unlike the majority of his psychoanalytic writing. It is also among the rare instances in his voluminous work in which Freud, a frequent presence in his own writings, is rebuffed by his interlocutor, unable to convince him of his case.

The essay Freud wrote for *Das Land Goethes,* "On Transience," described a literary version of a conversation he had had over the years with many people, including patients, poets, a princess, his daughter Anna, and his friends, the crux of which was a hoary metaphysical paradox: What value does life hold in the face of mortality, the certainty of extinction? It was the sort of "philosophical" question, like those pertaining to life after death, or the phenomena of the occult, that Freud typically rued as beyond the scope of scientific inquiry, beyond even the wisdom of poets, to whom he often deferred. Indeed, it falls to a "young but already famous" poet, Freud's adversary in this short dialogue, to question the value of mortal existence at all—an idea taken for granted by every human endeavor (and poetry above all), a premise whose affirmation every worldview, even that of science, accepts on faith as its point of departure.

Fear, uncertainty, and the privations of wartime had put Freud in a metaphysical cast of mind, and returned his attention to a problem that had long been the subject of his interest—the fate of pain and loss in human memory—a problem that now assumed greater poignancy. Pain and loss were apparent everywhere that winter, in the news, in his work, and at home. And the impending visit of an admired acquaintance soon gave new impetus to Freud's consideration of life's disappointments.

2

Perhaps the most representative poet of his era, René Maria Rilke was born in Prague in December 1875, the child of an unhappy marriage. The French femininity of his name brought him suffering in the military schools of his adolescence, where it seemed all too apt for the boy's slight frame and frailty. But it was also the name under which he began to write.

The young poet's first steps were halting and unfocused, and his early efforts at writing were interrupted with unenthusiastic preparations for careers in the military and then in law. While still unknown and unformed, Rilke met Lou Andreas-Salomé in May 1897 in the Munich salon of Jakob Wassermann, and was awed by the presence of the woman, almost fifteen years his senior, whose life and writing had already excited his imagination through her essay "Jesus the Jew." The smitten youth could hardly speak to her at this first meeting; but the following days found her barraged with letters importuning her for an audience, and before long, René had taken up residence not far from where she lived with her husband.

In Lou the young poet found his ideal companion, mother, lover, and muse, and under her tutelage he developed rapidly. She praised some of the works he eagerly showed her; more often she criticized his excesses, urging him to write more of the world he saw around him, and less of the abstract fairy tales inspired by his youthful feelings. She also encouraged Rilke, who had resisted university education, in his study of languages and history. Together they studied the art of Italy and Russia, attended plays and concerts, and took long walks in the German countryside near the summer home they came to share in Wolfratshausen, in the Isar valley.

In April 1898, at Lou's insistence, her lover went to Italy, where a lonely Rilke would keep a journal in the form of a dialogue with her. In the spring of the next year, Lou and René (together with her tolerant husband) set off on the first of two pilgrimages to Russia, a land they both idealized as pure, ancient, and pious.

Their experiences in Russia electrified the lovers, and would be remembered as the epitome of their affair. On a second trip there a year later, the pair visited Leo Tolstoy at his famous estate, Yasnaya Polyana, where they received a chilly reception that nevertheless became the stuff of legend—and not a little retrospective embellishment. Biographers agree that the visit paid to Tolstoy in 1900 was little more than a polite dismissal of two unknown and uninvited strangers by a renowned writer. Yet the accounts that preserve the visit in Lou's and Rilke's letters, memoirs, and fiction stage it as a scene of inspiration. The long hours the pair were forced to wait in a parlor of Tolstoy's home are ripe with excitement and expectation. A walk with the count through his fields becomes a pilgrimage, and the flowers he idly picks up and discards become emblems of art's harmony with nature (though in their actual conversation, he ridiculed lyrical poetry as worthless). Tolstoy's features are transmuted into those of a saint, like one of the painted, gilded icons Rilke admired in Russian art.

Years later, Rilke sought to turn the difficult encounter with the Russian master to profit as the culmination of his own novel *The Notebooks of Malte Laurids Brigge*. In two early drafts, his hero Malte confronts Tolstoy in what amounts to a face-off between art and reality or, nearly the same in this connection, between art and religion. In the first draft, the matter is put baldly, and offers a striking (if theological) echo of the young poet's sentiment in "On Transience": "If God exists then everything is already accomplished and we are melancholy, superfluous survivors for whom it makes no difference in which accidental way they will perish." The existence of God is reviled as the antithesis of artistic creation, depriving individual and artist of intention and the ability to create. It seems to take from him the right to his own death, one that can be made to bear the meaning the artist/individual desires for it. In Rilke's fictional construction, Tolstoy, rejecting art for God, opts for the greatest illusion of them all, choosing a world governed by divinity over one consecrated by artistic intention.

In a second draft, the threatening Tolstoy figure is reduced to a hysteric, whose suppression of his artistry has brought him only suffering, and even further suffering as he tries to make the world understand and conform to his choice. Here Tolstoy is a tragic figure, pathetically renouncing his artistic nature out of folly and weakness. Ultimately Rilke discarded both of these early drafts in favor of a retelling of the story of the Prodigal Son, in which Malte resigns himself to the necessary absence of love or, more precisely, to his inability to accept the love of others. The ending seemed to echo Rilke's own belief in the exclusive attention art demands of the artist—at the expense of his human relationships.

In the second draft, Rilke's hero wonders to himself at "what caused my mind to wander back to those May afternoons." The poet's meeting with Tolstoy had disappointed his expectations. But his expectations had taken on a life of their own, and become in his writing more alive to him than the reality of the encounter with Tolstoy. For Rilke, the events of that May afternoon at Yasnaya Polyana had become less a matter of realistic memory than of expectant imagination.

Rilke continued to speak of his meeting with Tolstoy for the rest of his life as a kind of initiation or milestone of his poetic development. However disappointing the actual visit with the legendary writer, the poetic revisions of the encounter held for Rilke an emotional truth more important to him than their historical reality.

During their Russian travels, Lou Salomé rechristened her protégé with a name that seemed to her more masculine, and more German, than his birth name. At her behest, René became Rainer. Rilke took evident pride in his new designation: "Rainer" is pronounced like *reiner,* German (and masculine) for "pure," and the poet, with his singular commitment to poetry, must have embraced the connection. Years later, he would use the adjective in the poetic epitaph he wrote for himself.

In Lou, Rilke had found the compass and polestar of his existence. But this role was not at all congenial to the fiercely independent writer, and she soon chafed under their arrangement.

In a later memoir, Lou recalled a postcard she had received from Rainer during their affair. The face of the postcard was completely black, darkened by the poet's ink, except for a star-shaped area near the top, through which white paper shone.

Lou thought it a gesture of vague tenderness, a romantic allusion to the celestial quality of their love, perhaps, or an intimation of the sidereal regard in which he held her.

But her suitor had something different in mind. The room he had rented during the fall of 1898 in the Berlin suburb of Schmargendorf was on the ground floor, facing the street. To hide their intimacy from the prying eyes of the city, the lovers would close the shutters, so that the only light that shone in entered through an aperture carved in the shutters. That opening was star-shaped, and cast light in its own image about the room, illuminating the pair as they embraced. It was this erotic image, the evocation of a real detail of their intimate hours framed in the shutter's starlight, that Rainer wished to recall to her senses with his postcard.

Lou termed this story of false constellations a light-hearted misunderstanding, but found in it something deeper, and troubling. She thought it a sign "evocative of their stars," of something between them incapable of expression, like the many lines in the letters between them that had been crossed through and blacked out by ink.

Near the end of his life, in his Fourth Duino Elegy, Rilke described what he saw as the paradoxical essence of loving:

> *But we, while we are intent upon one object,*
> *already feel the pull of another. Conflict*
> *is second nature to us. Aren't lovers*
> *always arriving at each other's boundaries?—*
> *although they promised vastness, hunting, home.*

15

Rilke believed that, in loving, lovers come closest to a higher, divine existence, and yet are impeded in this transcendence, precisely because they are distracted by their lover. The elegy was an expression of Rilke's enduring view that love was dangerous, since it interrupted the quest for self-perfection, through art. This idea—the precedence of artistic solitude over love and human connection—first took hold of him during the hours he spent studying with Lou, from their conversations and from her writings; after her rejection of him, Rilke made it his own and, through marriage, fatherhood, and countless affairs, never abandoned it.

The coming heartbreak was already in the air when Rilke sent his postcard, and the impending darkness colored his postal act of love. In blacking out everything except the memory of that star-shaped light, the poet saw what he wanted of his lover, and shut out the rest. He staked everything on his own singular memory, though it was only a snapshot or caricature of a life between them, as if their life together were a poem he might compose.

But Lou would not recognize herself in his starlight; she preferred to see herself free astride the heavens, in the inked night sky that engulfed the little white star, so insistent and demanding of her love. In producing such a moving, closely observed detail of their love, Rainer hoped to make of his memory a valentine for Lou. But she was already gone.

Not long after their return from Russia, in the later summer of 1900, Lou broke with the poet, asking him not to call or correspond with her except in his "direst" hour. She had sent him on his way, she said, because "it was necessary for you to enter into open spaces and freedom as quickly as possible, to develop everything within you fully." Lou's last lesson for Rilke was a harsh one: His progress as an artist lay in solitude, and without her.

Less than a year later, in April 1901, Rilke, as Rainer, married Clara Westhoff, a sculptor he had met only weeks after the break with Lou, during a visit to an artists' colony at Worpswede in the damp moor country north of Berlin. Nearly from the outset, Rilke felt confined by the union, and after barely a year—one that saw the birth of their only child, Ruth—the couple began to live apart, she in Germany and he eventually in Paris. Rilke embarked on a peripatetic existence that left him chronically unsettled, constantly in love, and routinely out of sorts.

For more than two years after their break, Rilke and Lou had no contact, and they were not to see each other again for some five years. When Lou finally met Clara Rilke, after a plea from Rilke, the two women took instantly to each other, and Lou soon made the younger woman, as she did many others, her protégée and ward. She demonstrated an active interest in the waning marriage, and especially in the welfare of Ruth, who lived most of the time with her mother's parents. At one point, Lou even recommended to Clara that she enlist the police in her efforts to exact child support from Rilke.

17

Rainer responded to Lou's suggestion with a vehement defense of his life as an artist. He argued that his duty to art exceeded all other obligations, including those to his family, because it involved the creation of something larger than all of them, a world of beauty where they would live together, a world free of need.

Through the turbulence of his personal life, the poet honed his craft. Almost every year from 1894, when he turned nineteen, through the first years of the new century, Rilke published a new volume of his work, which from its tentative, florid beginnings gradually found its way toward his mature style—hermetic, solipsistic, allusive, evasive—and to an audience that grew wider with each new effort, particularly after the publication of his *New Poems,* in 1907.

After the eventful years of his affair with Lou, and the subsequent interlude of his marriage and honeymoon in Worpswede, Rilke received a commission to write a monograph on the work of Auguste Rodin. In August 1902, he moved to Paris, where he eventually became the sculptor's personal secretary. In Paris, Rilke established himself as a poet, and it was there that he began the work that would consume his next several years, *The Notebooks of Malte Laurids Brigge,* a fractured, fictional portrait of his youth, and the work for which, with the *Duino Elegies,* the *Sonnets to Orpheus,* and the avuncular *Letters to a Young Poet,* Rilke is perhaps best known to the world.

In 1910, Rilke finished *The Notebooks of Malte Laurids Brigge,* and the voice of his inspiration grew still. To hear it again, the poet moved restlessly through the world. He followed El Greco to Toledo, hoping to find in the painter's vision some clue to his own. In a chauffeured car borrowed from Princess Marie von Thurn und Taxis, he wandered Europe, through Avignon, Cannes, Sanremo, and Bologna. From the deck of a steamship he surveyed the Nile and Egypt's monuments. Asleep beneath the palm shade in Tunis, he dreamed of the Orient. But even as the world in all its beauty became real before his traveler's eyes, without poetry his own spirit seemed to dissolve. Absent the chorus of words that gave his life meaning, he wrote, he had become "improbable" to himself. His life was a wild turbulence of romance and foreign winds, but behind it lay an emptiness more terrible than death.

After years of silence and strain between them, Rilke turned to Lou in despair. They resumed their relationship, though now in a platonic, more distant form. But its essential character remained: Rilke suffered; Lou consoled, from a distance.

In early 1912, in the terror brought on by depression, and desperate to restore his failed inspiration, Rilke turned hopefully to psychoanalysis. He wrote to Lou, who in the meantime had become an analyst, for advice, and she enthusiastically recommended another analyst, named Gebsattel (who, in keeping with the intimate, even hothouse climate that prevailed in early psychoanalytic circles, was also her lover). Rilke wrote to Gebsattel, but then wavered; he was afraid analysis would clean him up, correct the flaws of his personality in "red ink like a child's exercise in school." Again he sought guidance from Lou, who now reversed herself: she urged him to follow his own heart and not pursue the treatment, which she, too, feared would pose a threat to his creative powers.

Although Rilke's inspiration returned long enough for him to begin the *Duino Elegies,* a project that would take a decade to complete, it vanished again as quickly as it had appeared. The crisis would recur again and again in the poet's life over the next decade: when unable to write, Rilke lost his way, became "improbable" to himself, and plunged into depression. When he and Lou met in Munich in September 1913, it was to help the poet find what he had lost. Two years later, in similar circumstances, he turned to Freud.

On the Monday before Christmas of 1915, Rilke visited Freud and his family at their home at Berggasse 19. The poet was temporarily stationed in Vienna, having been drafted into military service as a war historian. He was miserable; he had bitterly hated army life in the military academies of his youth; now again in uniform, he worked frantically to obtain a discharge, to return to the life of independence he believed his poetry demanded.

But that evening, the poet was "charming company. You would also get along with him very easily," Freud remarked in a letter to his friend and fellow analyst Sándor Ferenczi, who was stationed in a remote region of Hungary as a garrison doctor.

Soon after this visit, in February 1916, in his only known letter to Freud, Rilke wrote how his military experience was affecting him, and confided his hesitant wish to talk more personally with the psychoanalyst. "First for fourteen days I was in training, which ended with my resulting dispatch to the War Archive, where I serve interminable office hours, as mute now in spirit as I was before in body. I was often on the point of helping myself up out of the depths by having a talk with you. But finally the decision prevailed to struggle through alone, as far as one still has a miserable shred of solitude left. If I can gradually get some measure of control, then I shall certainly invite myself and come to see you; I know that will be good for me."

Freud invited the poet for another visit, but Rilke's first was to be his last. A month later Freud wrote to Lou: "Ernst [Freud's son] . . . has at last met his hero Rilke. But not at our house. Rilke was not to be persuaded to visit us a second time, though his first visit . . . had been so very cordial."

In July, Freud learned from Lou that Rilke had been discharged from military service and had returned to Munich, where he would wait out the war. For the poet, it was to be another bleak period, a time when, because of the conflict, he could no longer travel to Italy, Spain, or France, or flee to the aristocratic castle refuges he had enjoyed before 1914. Never alone amid the chaos and crowded barracks of wartime, he was unable to settle himself into the work he felt burning inside him now.

Freud responded to the news of Rilke's departure in a letter to Lou that expressed his sense of injury. Rilke, "whom I should like to congratulate on having regained his poetic freedom, made it quite clear to us in Vienna that 'no lasting [bond] can be forged with him.' Cordial as he was on his first visit, we have not been able to persuade him to pay us a second."

Lou sought to reassure Freud of her friend's intentions. "No, do not misinterpret Rainer's attitude. It was not due to any estrangement on his part, but only to his shattered state of mind. I know quite well what he really feels about you."

Yet whatever it was that Rilke felt about Freud, the two men did not meet again. What more they knew of each other they knew through the continued mediation of Lou Salomé.

3

Lou Andreas-Salomé was born Louise von Salomé in St. Petersburg in February 1861, the daughter of a general with the ear of Tsar Alexander II. She was raised in a prominent household of German descent and strict religion, and the themes that would shape her life made themselves felt before she was seventeen. Determined to pursue her education in a society that thought it was wasted on a woman, the teenaged Lou became the pupil of Hendrik Gillot, an influential Lutheran pastor and tutor to the tsar's children. In a pattern that would become familiar for her, Gillot fell in love with her, risking both family and career, and she rejected him. She fled the stifling conservatism of Moscow for Zurich, and enrolled in one of the few universities in Europe that at the time accepted women. Soon she was traveling throughout the continent, making an impression on everyone she met, and especially on Friedrich Nietzsche.

In 1882, the twenty-one-year-old Lou traveled to Italy, in hopes of restoring her fragile health, in the company of her mother. In Rome, Lou was introduced to the atheist and philosopher Paul Rée, and through him to his close friend Nietzsche. The three of them entered into a complex *folie à trois* that played itself out, largely through letters, over the course of a dramatic year that began with awakening intimacies and ended in bitterness and recriminations that established Lou's enduring notoriety as the thinking man's femme fatale.

In a famous photograph of the three, Nietzsche and Rée are each harnessed by an arm to a small cart into which Lou crouches, a nervous smile on her face and a makeshift whip in her hand. Rée's smile is uncertain as Nietzsche leans lustily toward him, nearly grinning beneath his collar of a mustache. The image, odd even in our jaded age, was outrageous in its own, and is widely read as an ironic reversal of the philosopher's admonition, in *Thus Spoke Zarathustra*: "You are going to women? Do not forget the whip!"

The picture was taken—in Lucerne, in the summer of 1882—to the chagrin of the photographer, and indeed, of everyone involved, except Nietzsche. Early that afternoon, in the Löwengarten he had proposed marriage, for a second time, to the young Russian, who for a second time refused him. Both proposal and refusal were anticipated by all three members of the odd ménage that had formed earlier that year in Rome. There, in the drawing room of the renowned Wagnerian, revolutionary, and suffragist Malwida von Meysenbug, Lou met Rée, with whom she felt an instant rapport. Their clandestine (and, for a well-bred girl of that era, wildly inappropriate) perambulations through the Roman nighttime soon transformed Rée's feelings for his companion into ardor, and it was not long before she found herself in the familiar position of refusing his proposal of marriage.

Instead, Lou proposed an unconventional arrangement: With a third, male companion, they would live together in a paradise of intellectual fraternity, learning from and teaching one another. Willing to take what he could get from his elusive *innamorata*, Rée thought immediately of his friend Nietzsche.

Nietzsche was quick to warm to the plan, and, before even meeting her, he sensed the seeds of his destiny in this young Russian. He had spent the winter isolated in Genoa, prostrate with insomnia, pain, opium, and loneliness, and overwhelmed by the revelation of eternal recurrence, the doctrine he would soon elaborate, which held that humans are condemned to repeat in unending cycles the great themes of history. Having sailed to Sicily in search of better weather for his health, he was soon driven out in search of greener pastures by the blasting sirocco.

After a flurry of letters—including, conveyed through Rée, a first matrimonial offer—he appeared before Lou and Rée in a secluded corner of St. Peter's Basilica (where Rée worked with gleeful malice on a refutation of God), in plain, worn clothes and with near-blind eyes which, Lou wrote, "lent his features a quite special magic. . . . They looked . . . inwards as if into the distance."

On a whirlwind journey up through Italy in the company of Rée, Lou, and her puritanical mother (who vainly fought her daughter's intentions every step of the way), Nietzsche grew increasingly enamored of the young Russian, and a mysterious afternoon the two spent together atop Sacro Monte near the northern Lake Orta seemed to him to set the seal of fate upon their union.

Not long after this trip, Nietzsche asked for the meeting with Lou in the Löwengarten, where his marriage proposal was refused a second time. The eventual consequences of this refusal on their relationship, and on Nietzsche's mental state, would be catastrophic, but that afternoon Nietzsche gaily proposed that the trio have their photograph taken and later visit Richard Wagner's old home by Lake Lucerne, where the philosopher had spent many happy times.

In July of the same year, Lou visited Nietzsche in his family home in the woods of Tautenburg. The pair spent three long weeks in intellectual communion, during which time Lou, who was sixteen years younger than the philosopher, "definitely [grew] a few inches," as Rée later put it to Nietzsche.

But the idyll did not last. As the intimacy among them grew, the designs of each of the three friends on the others showed themselves to be incompatible. Each of her horsemen came to view Lou as his ordained bride, and to this end they each began to compete for her exclusive affection. In her turn, Lou hoped that the unruly emotions of the one would keep the other at bay, that she could live out her platonic study fantasy unencumbered by the weight of the men's desires accompanying her at every step.

Worse, Lou had made a powerful enemy in Nietzsche's sister Elisabeth. Jealous of her brother's love and horrified by her rival's scandalous behavior, the future anti-Semite and Nazi propagandist directed her considerable powers of vengeance against Lou, in hopes of turning Nietzsche and indeed all of polite society against her.

As the dispute escalated from its beginnings in jealous intrigues, the relations among the perfect friends deteriorated into wholesale animosity. Rée, Nietzsche, Lou, Elisabeth, and their respective supporters hurled denunciations and insults at one another, and the true picture of precipitating events gradually disappeared beneath the accumulation of accusation and rumor. In the end, which came less than a year after the whole affair started, Nietzsche's friendship with Rée lay in ruins, and after living some months longer with Rée, Lou went by herself to Berlin, never again to speak to either man.

Nietzsche credited Lou von Salomé with inspiring *Thus Spoke Zarathustra*: "If I do not hit on an alchemical trick for turning even this—dung into gold I am lost. . . . My relations with Lou are now in their last, painful throes," Nietzsche wrote his friend Franz Overbeck at Christmas 1882, in the aftermath of the affair; during ten days in January 1883, in a state he described as trancelike, he produced the first part of the work. Toward the end of this first part, the prophet/hero encounters an old woman, who decries before him the faults of her gender. It is here, from the mouth of the old woman, that one hears the appalling if comic dictum "You are going to women? Do not forget the whip!"

The first book of *Thus Spoke Zarathustra* has a frenetic quality, reflecting its genesis in the author's turmoil over his catastrophic love affair. In his relations with Lou, he had sought the "clear sky" of a perfect understanding between them, free of suspicion and doubt, to accord with the sense of intellectual union that their three weeks together at Tautenburg had inspired in him. The folly of this wish, tantamount to the childish demand that the world conform to one's own expectations, was, he felt, a worthy object of Zarathustra's derision; like his author and parent, Zarathustra found himself an outcast among those he loved.

By the time of the publication of Lou's first novel, Nietzsche's emotions had cooled enough that he could praise the work—which was based in part on their experience together—as "serious." But he had not forgotten the hurt that she had dealt him. He described Lou to a friend with an epithet that would follow her for the rest of her life: "And if it is certainly not the Eternal-Feminine that draws this girl onward, perhaps it is the Eternal-Masculine." The comment cruelly parodies Goethe's famous notion of the "eternal feminine," often used as a metaphor for creative inspiration. Nietzsche's parody implied either that Lou was more interested in chasing men than she was in her work, or that she herself was more man than woman.

After her transformative experience with Nietzsche and Rée, Lou embarked on a writing career that provided her at long last with the independence she desired. She rose to prominence with her book *Friedrich Nietzsche in seinen Werken* (*Friedrich Nietzsche in His Works*) the first to be written on the philosopher. Over the next decade, she gained a wider audience through her fiction (she would write eight novels and nearly two dozen long stories, most of them semiautobiographical narratives involving resolute heroines in determined search of personal freedom) and through forceful writings on spirituality and religion. At the time of her first encounter with Freud, she was widely considered the most important female writer in Germany. Indeed, by 1913, "Frau Lou"—as she was known throughout the German literary world—was more famous than Rilke or even Freud.

Lou was welcomed in literary salons across Europe, especially in Germany, where, through her work and rumor both (the latter fueled by such avid detractors as Elisabeth Nietzsche), she soon became very well known. Courted unsuccessfully by many prominent men, Lou settled in the end on an unlikely suitor, Friedrich Carl Andreas, a scholar of Persian culture, who answered her refusals of marriage by plunging a knife into his chest before her eyes, coming literally within an inch of his life to convince her of his passion. Lou relented and married him, but the ensuing union was on her own, unusual terms, and remained, apparently, unconsummated for its over-forty-year duration. In the meantime, Lou Andreas-Salomé, as she was henceforth known, continued her campaign of erotic conquest throughout literary Europe. In the course of twenty years after her wedding, the procession of her lovers was rumored to include such literary luminaries as the playwright Richard Beer-Hoffman, Arthur Schnitzler, and, most famous, the young Rilke. Beginning with a novel in which she detailed in thin disguise her experiences with Gillot, her pastor teacher, Lou memorialized her exploits in her fiction and memoirs; she was in turn memorialized by her lovers. The result of this cross-pollination is an ambiguous record, in which the truth of historical events is filtered through each writer's own recollections.

Even before meeting Freud, Lou showed a keen interest in analysis. Freud first learned personally of her in 1912, in a letter from Carl Gustav Jung, to whom she had submitted a paper on sublimation—the analytic theory of creativity. Jung regarded her and her paper with skepticism, yet, knowing her fame, he told Freud that her support would be an important step to the "secularization" of psychoanalysis. Despite Jung's reservations, "Frau Lou" was invited to attend the weekly meetings of the Vienna Psycho-analytical Society.

The Wednesday meetings routinely drew a motley crowd to Freud's house at Berggasse 19. In addition to the psychiatrists and other physicians (who, like Freud, had come to psychoanalysis through medicine), the gathering included lawyers, art historians, philosophers, and musicians. Convening after dinner, visitors were sustained by the desserts, coffee, and wine proffered by Freud's wife, Martha, and continued late into the evening, often until two a.m. One member of the group opened each evening with a presentation, suggesting analytic interpretations of subjects ranging from folklore to politics to the music of Wagner; these would be followed by discussion, anchored by the anticipated remarks of the host. Soon, Freud found himself directing his remarks exclusively toward Lou's chair—a habit he realized only the first time it sat empty.

The minutes of the first meeting Lou attended, which was devoted to an analysis by Freud himself of the dream of a twenty-three-year-old woman, record no comments by the new arrival; in fact, during the seven months she regularly attended, she spoke very little at the formal, sometimes contentious gatherings. But when she was alone with Freud, things were different. On the warm spring evenings when he accompanied her to her hotel, at the dinners she enjoyed with his family, and after her return to Berlin, through their frequent letters, the two discussed psychoanalysis at length, and much else besides. Lou talked to him of Nietzsche (of whom Freud once said, "He who wants to be original as a psychoanalyst should not have read Nietzsche"), and Russia, and Rilke; Freud spoke to her of his family, of his children's admiration for Rilke, and of his youngest child, Anna, whom Lou would later befriend.

They spoke also of beauty and nature, and especially of the mysterious nature of love, which Lou had long struggled to define in her tangled life as well as in her work. Through analysis, Lou came to see love, beauty, nature, and death as products of the elemental urges of the "libido" that Freud's work insisted drove all human action, and at whose base lay the infantile need to love, to be loved, and to destroy what stood in the way.

It was this promise of revelation, the promise to unlock the ancient doors, that drew Lou to psychoanalysis and Freud. The attraction was mutual. In a letter to Sándor Ferenczi shortly before the end of her stay in Vienna, Freud appraised his new acquaintance: "She is a highly significant woman, even though all the tracks around her go into the lion's den but none come out." In his remark, an allusion to one of Aesop's fables, Freud's admiration is tinged with curiosity and, perhaps, excitement, before this woman whose interests, he pointedly assured Ferenczi, "were really of a purely intellectual nature."

Three years later, in a letter to Freud written in June 1916, Lou summarized her experience of the Wednesday meetings, her view of psychoanalysis, and her place in it. "I would like to have got up at the end to thank psycho-analysis for the fact that it leads us away from the isolated work at our desks into vital activity and into a kind of brotherhood. Just as . . . it established the absolute integrity of the individual, so it also brings about a close connection between all those working in this field, and this can in certain circumstances lead to a somewhat lively interchange of views. If only . . . honesty to oneself and others . . . remains untarnished, then—at least in a woman's eyes—all is well, and it is a joy to see even 'brothers' thus engaged in mutual conflict. . . . In this way the decree as to what befits the two sexes in the world is properly fulfilled: men do battle, women offer thanks."

CHAPTER TWO

I*n 1915,* the year of Rilke's visit to Berggasse 19 and of the writing of "On Transience," Freud was completing work on his theory of mourning, which he would first set before the public in the essay. The concept of the work of mourning (*Trauerarbeit*) was a major advance in psychoanalytic theory, and it came against a backdrop of gathering shadows cast by the war, and of other, more immediate losses and conflicts in Freud's world.

His new ideas grew out of his recent work on narcissism, and together with that work were the seeds of what would become known in psychoanalysis as "object relations." The essential premise of object relations theory is that every sexual instinct seeks an "object"—the lover—to whom it looks for its satisfaction. According to Freud, the prototypes for the choice of a love object are established very early in infancy, and have only two sources. The two kinds of objects—two basic blueprints for love—are the "anaclitic" and the "narcissistic." The former refers to the objects that resemble those on whom we depend as children for our care (*anaclitic* means, literally, "depending on" or "hanging on to"). The latter refers to objects who resemble ourselves, echoing the time early in our infancy when we took pleasure and satisfaction from sources within our own bodies.

From these two templates, or some combination of them, Freud believed we base our object choice—a theoretical way to describe falling in love. It is in this sense that he says, "The finding of an object is the refinding of it." Love is the repetition of one's history of love, either love for early caregivers or love of ourselves, or, most likely, a combination of both; for there are no "pure" object choices, exclusively anaclitic or narcissistic. For Freud, the way we love reflects the entire history of our development.

To the extent that an object is anaclitic, it is an incarnation in the present, external world of the "internalized" objects of our past—typically, our parents, and those nannies, teachers, siblings, and other important models who have followed in their footsteps. These internalized objects—the traces or memories of others that live on within us—are the basis for all subsequent relations with others *as others*: in much the same way a person cannot make sense of another's speech without first understanding a common language, these inner objects form the basis for all our subsequent interactions with new "objects"— with the real people who will populate the grown-up infant's world, inside and out.

When an object is narcissistic, it is a reproduction in the external world of oneself, or some element of oneself; in other words, it is a person/object in which one recognizes something of oneself. In all such cases, the object the lover seeks is a version of himself. More accurate, the lover seeks some reminder in the world to rekindle the omnipotent bliss of his infancy, when he believes himself to be the center of the universe, able to satisfy his every need with a cry, a wish, or a whisper—when the whole world is a fantasy in which pleasure and satisfaction are taken for granted, just as a well-nurtured infant takes for granted his satisfaction in the ministrations of his mother (whose body, in his earliest existence, the baby cannot distinguish from his own).

For Freud, in normal development, this type of "object love" is the source of feelings of fraternity, patriotism, and philanthropy. But in pathological cases, the lover shares the shriveled fate of Oscar Wilde's Dorian Gray, or of the mythical Narcissus himself, wasting away before his own image, unable to sustain himself by a love that can never be reciprocated except as reflection. Because the narcissistic love object is not, in the end, himself, the lover must always be disappointed.

Freud said that only one force opposed the dangerous excesses of self-love: "Limitation of narcissism can, according to our theoretical views, only be produced by one factor, a libidinal tie with other people. Love for oneself knows only one barrier—love for others, love for objects." It is as though a person has a store of love, like a bank account, whose resources can be allocated. Inevitably conflicts arise between these competing forces, between narcissistic love of oneself and love of others. Also, it is possible to hate those we love while loving them nonetheless, as Freud points out, quoting Alcibiades in Plato's *Symposium*: "Many a time have I wished that he were dead, and yet I know that I should be much more sorry than glad if he were to die: so that I am at my wits' end." For every human, then, love is a constant, warlike struggle within, between us and them; taking both sides, we lose either way.

Freud's views on narcissism dramatically altered his theories about love in general. In his early psychoanalytic thinking, he had seen love as an outgrowth of an infant's satisfaction and need; from the pleasures of nurture, we grew to love our mother, then our father, then anyone who resembled them. Later, with his theory of narcissism, Freud recognized the importance of the even earlier pleasure we took from ourselves, initially endowed as we are with the apparently boundless, if illusory, capacity to satisfy our own needs.

In *Civilization and Its Discontents*, Freud linked love to this earliest state of satisfaction. When the libido finds its object—when we fall in love—the result, he said, is a blending of self and world, a return to the first state of infancy, which he would eventually characterize as an "oceanic" feeling. Earlier, in *Beyond the Pleasure Principle*, Freud had returned to Aristophanes' account of love in the *Symposium*. According to this famous allegory, humans originally contained within them both sexes, man and woman. These ur-humans were subsequently divided into their two gendered halves, and were afterward destined to seek out what they had lost in their division. Freud reminded us of this allegory to suggest that the roots of sexuality lie in what he called a "death-drive": By the ecstasy of sexual exchange, we seek to return to a biologically earlier state of being—of union or fusion—and so to be, in a sense, born again.

When Aristophanes speaks of conjoined sexes, he truly means conjoined people, body, soul, and spirit. It is a curious vision, for how can two entities coexist in a single body? But it is also compelling, and remains fairly representative of contemporary ideas of romantic love.

The allegory says that love is destiny and origin, past and future. It makes of our present a transient, difficult way station between what was and what will be. Like religious salvation, it takes the burden of love off our shoulders, makes it neither heroic nor accidental but natural and destined, even down to our choice of partner. The complementary human genitalia become the locks and keys of the single door meant to be opened onto a perfect communication between two people (a man and a woman), affirming at once both the redemption of our own individuality, and the abolition of our isolation from others.

With this allegory, Freud breaks off the "speculative" discussion that introduces the "death-drive." He says a great deal in *Beyond the Pleasure Principle* that others have found difficult to accept—most important, that there is a force within us in opposition to our will to live, a force that strives to return to the inanimate origin of all species. What he does not say, but only implies, may be even harder to bear. Because with the idea of sexual love as a return to the original union, Freud denies the individuality of love; he even deprives it of its vitality. In this conception, love's goal is not reproduction so much as exhaustion, the disbursal of the sexual forces in order to return to an earlier state of union—union with inanimate matter. Love is the path back to death.

In an early draft of "Mourning and Melancholia," the essay (begun before "On Transience" but published after its appearance in *Das Land Goethes*) in which Freud most fully explained his ideas about mourning, he described how in the "normal" course of grief the mourner gradually detaches his capacity for love (his "libido") from the lost love object. In doing this, his capacity for love (which Freud imagined as a kind of quantifiable emotional energy) returns to its source within him, carrying along with it into his unconscious world an image of the vanished object, which then becomes a part of him. Freud evoked this complicated, hard-to-imagine journey of the love object from outside to inside the mourner with a poetic, elusive phrase: "The shadow of the object falls across the ego and obscures it." It is a slow process, the detachment achieved only piece by piece, and in concluding the essay, Freud acknowledged that it remained a mystery to him why the process was so painful.

Painful, but imperative. The consequences of refusing to mourn, of refusing to let go of the lost love object, are dire. Going further than he would in the essay's published version, Freud predicted the result of an inability to mourn, which he calls "melancholia," to be a "hallucinatory wish psychosis." Unable to mourn the loss of the love object, the bereft turns his back on reality, and is trapped in a world of his own making.

Although Freud would later mute the connection between the inability to mourn and psychosis, it was the failure to face the reality of grief that he believed barred the young poet and his taciturn friend from appreciating the beauty that surrounded them.

2

Freud's initial investigations into the nature of love, loss, and mourning coincided with the disastrous end of his close friendship with Carl Jung. By 1912, Jung had gone his own way, forcefully and with vengeance, by rejecting the heart of psychoanalytic theory, the theory of sexuality. While the controversy between Freud and Jung concerned theoretical matters, the exchange could not have been more personal; Anna Freud later remembered that the summer of 1913, just before their final break, was the only time she could remember her father depressed.

Freud's and Jung's letters of 1912 and 1913 ring with accusations of infidelity and egoism—a sad pageant of the frustrations that led to their eventual break. Their friendship, built up since 1907 on a foundation of intellectual admiration and personal affection, in decline blurred the personal and the psycho-analytic; confusing arguments over the importance of Freud's libido theory with petty disputes, such as that over the "Kreuzlingen gesture" (Freud, though visiting a sick friend, had professed himself unable to see his heir apparent at his nearby vacation place of Kreuzlingen; Jung took this as a personal snub). By September 8, 1913, at the opening bell of the Fourth International Psycho-analytical Congress in Munich, it was over. The two men did not speak to each other at all during the Congress, and they never met again.

Jung's rebellion against Freud and his theories had been long brewing. In his memoirs, Jung recalled the initial moment of discord between the two men, in 1909, while aboard an ocean liner bound for a lecture tour of the United States (it would be Freud's only visit). The two men were, in the custom of the early days of psychoanalysis, analyzing each other's dreams. Freud recounted a dream he had had the night before, and Jung asked for a further detail, so that he might hit upon an interpretation. Freud demurred, as Jung remembered it, saying that such a personal disclosure "would risk my authority." For Jung, Freud's reticence was a painful, paternal rebuke, and the beginning of the end of their friendship.

The two also discussed a dream Jung had had during the crossing. He had dreamt he was in an old house, with three stories, each furnished differently. The top floor was in a baroque style, the second in a medieval one. When he reached the basement, Jung found a hole to yet another level, where he saw two skulls. Freud believed the skulls represented a death wish in

Jung against his intimates, and inquired of the younger man who he thought the skulls might represent. Jung replied, dutifully and deceptively, that they must have stood for his wife and his sister-in-law.

But as he recounted later in his memoirs, Jung did not really believe the skulls represented a death wish. Instead, the dream eventually became the cornerstone of his new "analytic psychology." In this new scheme, the house would represent the various stages of man, and the two skulls man's prehistory, one representing *Homo erectus* (who eventually died out) and the other *Homo sapiens* (who became humans), both reflecting the fates of man's ancestors.

The differences between Freud's and Jung's versions of the dream underscored the theoretical differences that would tear them apart. For Jung, the impulses that Freud believed were the source of all motivation—libido (sexual energy) and aggression—and which led him to interpret Jung's dream as containing a death wish, were only expressions of a broad, universally shared life force Jung would later call the "anima," which joined all beings who ever lived, in the past, present, and future, as he believed his dream demonstrated.

But that evening together on the ship, Jung lied to Freud, certain that Freud could never accept such an interpretation. Jung knew this because the friends had already disagreed on the scientific plausibility of ghosts. Earlier in the year, in March, Jung had visited Freud in Vienna, and in Freud's office the two had engaged in a heated debate about the veracity of occult phenomena. While Jung, an advocate of the paranormal, was driv-

ing home his point, the men heard a loud noise behind a book-
case, which Jung described as a poltergeist. Freud denied the
supernatural origin of the noise, but Jung correctly predicted
the mysterious sound's recurrence. Freud was, reluctantly,
convinced.

Yet in a letter written soon after Jung's visit, Freud renewed
his skepticism: "My credulity, or at least my willingness to believe, vanished with the magic of your personal presence; once
again, for some inward reasons that I can't put my finger on, it
strikes me as quite unlikely that such phenomena should exist;
I confront the de-spiritualized furniture as the poet confronted
undeified Nature after the gods of Greece had passed away."
Freud recalled a superstition he had held concerning the year of
his death—a superstition he eventually analyzed as a symptom
of his own neurosis. The notion had asserted itself during a trip
he took with his brother Alexander to Greece in 1904, and
Freud concluded that, with such superstitions, one begins to
see everywhere confirmation of what one wants to believe; quoting Mephistopheles' description of inebriation from Goethe's
Faust, he observed that "one sees Helen [of Troy] in every
woman." Though playful, the dispute underscored the growing
tension between Freud's secular rationalism and Jung's nascent
mysticism.

During yet another argument with Jung, but before the
crossing to America, Freud had fainted. Although he waved it
away as a physical symptom of exhaustion, he was aware of the
ambivalence toward Jung that the act betrayed. At his last
meeting with Jung before the 1913 Psycho-analytical Congress

formally ended their friendship, Freud fainted again. Jung lifted him to a couch in an adjoining room, where, upon reviving, Freud dazedly gasped, *"Es muss süss sein zu sterben"*—It must be sweet to die. His words echo Sophocles' Antigone:

> *How sweet to die in such pursuit! to rest*
> *Loved by him whom I have loved*
> *Sinner of a holy sin, with longer time*
> *To charm the dead than those who live, for I*
> *Shall abide forever there.*

Freud's poignant outburst expressed torn feelings. On the one hand, he seemed to embrace death itself, to end the misery into which his troubled friendship had plunged him; on the other, he yearned to linger in the arms of his trusted friend, and die himself rather than see their affection perish.

Jung was only the latest in a line of Freud's doomed friendships. Wilhelm Fliess—Freud's closest friend from 1890 to 1901, in whom he confided during the period of his self-analysis and the writing of his most famous work, *The Interpretation of Dreams*—grew jealous and distant after the publication of Freud's book, and even accused him of plagiarism. After a distant exchange in 1904, the two never spoke to each other again. Wilhelm Stekel and Alfred Adler also joined and later abandoned the psychoanalytic movement, as in his own way did Freud's intimate friend Sándor Ferenczi. These defections so troubled Freud that he eventually gave his blessing to the formation of a secret "Committee" of those loyal to him and his ideas, whose mission was to protect the fledgling psychoanalytic movement against future dissent. In time, this effort was undone, in no small part thanks to the departure of Otto Rank, Freud's longtime secretary and protégé.

Of such defectors from the psychoanalytic movement, Freud would remark: "The truth is that these people have picked out a few cultural overtones from the symphony of life and have once more failed to hear the mighty and primordial melody of the instincts." Freud believed they were deaf, or at least profoundly resistant, to the essential insight of psychoanalysis, that behavior is motivated by the dislocated desires of the libido.

Elsewhere, in *The Interpretation of Dreams,* Freud gave a more personal explanation for his volatile friendships. "I have always required an intimate friend and a hated enemy—often in the same person." The source of these turbulent affections was also clear to him: "My warm friendships as well as my enmities with contemporaries went back to my relations in childhood with a nephew who was a year my senior. . . . All my friends have in a certain sense been reincarnations of this first figure who long since have appeared before my troubled gaze. They have been *revenants.*" Freud's relationships, no less than those of his patients, were haunted by ghosts of the past.

CHAPTER THREE

Freud and Rilke first met in early September 1913 in Munich, at the Bayerischer Hof hotel, site of the Fourth International Psycho-analytical Congress and the last act of the friendship and intellectual adventure shared by Freud and Jung.

Outside, the streets were in humid disarray, bathed in a sunlit urban haze. The summer air was thick with talk of the political storm gathering within Austria-Hungary; the world beyond the crowded streets would hold together less than a year.

But in the Paradengasse, among the resplendent halls of the Bayerischer Hof, the uncertain future seemed dully abstract. The Hof had been built in 1840 to house noble visitors to the imperial palace across the street, and its gilded ornaments, though not a century old, shone like artifacts from a mythic past, bearing no trace of the depths of the turmoil that would soon bring down the German empire. Freud and Rilke met there in the lobby, beneath the crafted chandeliers. Rilke had

come in the company of his friend and onetime lover, Lou
Andreas-Salomé. Freud was surrounded by his lieutenants,
who gladly made room for the illustrious new arrivals, especially the enigmatic Frau Lou.

In other circumstances, Freud and Rilke, both raised in rela-
tive privation, might have reveled in the opulence of the Bayerischer Hof. But the Munich congress was rife with tension, the
analysts' loyalties divided along national and intellectual lines;
the large rooms of the hotel were like field camps for the bat-
tling factions, Swiss, German, and Austrian, all brought to a
head by the rancor between Freud and Jung.

It was here, among the elegance and chaos, that Freud met
Rilke. In her journal entry for September 7–8, Lou remembered the encounter: "I was delighted to bring Rainer to Freud,
they liked each other, and we stayed together that evening until late at night." Rilke would have had to conceal his distaste
for smoke in the presence of Freud's ubiquitous cigars, as well
as his own jealousies, for two of Lou's recent lovers (Viktor von
Gebsattel and Viktor Tausk) were at the Congress that evening.
What Freud, Rilke, and Lou discussed can only be surmised;
Lou's journal offers no further hint of the meeting, and no
other record exists. Hours later, the two men parted company
for the evening, and nearly for good, destined to see each other
only once more, two years later, in the midst of war.

On the afternoon after that first encounter with Rilke, Freud
walked with Frau Lou in one of Munich's public gardens,
where they discussed the plausibility of telepathy (the very

same question that had prompted Freud's initial dispute with Jung).

Only weeks before, in August, Freud had been in San Martino di Castrozza, in the Dolomites, for his summer holiday. The 1912 Baedeker's guide for South Tyrol (which Freud, who had already spent several summers with his family in the region, may very well have had with him on his holiday) offers a breathless description of the surroundings. The mountains' "unique character resides in the sharp individualism of their masses: bare, steep falling walls beside bright valleys and high plateaus; fantastic, wild clefted [heights] with pinnacles and towers; a wealth of mutable images of pure space."

Named for the mineral of which they are formed, the Dolomites were renowned for their inspiring beauty. Arthur Schnitzler (a favorite writer of Freud's) praised the region for its air "like Champagne." In a town not far away stood the solitary hut to which Gustav Mahler returned from New York in the summers, and in which he composed his last symphonies; in his memory Richard Strauss rendered these mountains—their storms and dawns, nights and transformations—into music, in his *Alpine Symphony*.

In 1913 sovereignty over the Dolomites was divided between Italy and Austria. Having changed hands during the wars of the twentieth century, the region is now officially Italian, but it retains the character of a crossroads that was a regular feature of Europe's days of empire.

In other summers the Freud family had stayed in Klobenstein, to the north, and for several summers in nearby Lavarone, which Baedeker termed "a place for air cures, of hills, meadows, and densely forested plateaus by a small lake." This year the Freuds chose San Martino di Castrozza, "an alpine hospice, founded in the twelfth century, now sought as a resort, [which lies] in a richly wooded hollow opening to the south," with wide views as far as the peaks of the Vette di Feltre range which by evening light glow a magnificent red." Freud's family had arrived ahead of him, and in the weeks leading up to his arrival, his daughter Anna sent him letters imploring him to hurry, painting for her father splendid images of what awaited him there.

Today one can navigate the Dolomites more or less easily by car, but in 1913 the journey from Vienna was arduous. From the Westbahnhof, one took the train, for a trip lasting many hours, to nearby Bozen (Bolzano), and there boarded a hired carriage. A carriage ride was a rare pleasure for Freud's children; his son Martin later remembered how the rattling wheels both soothed and excited him and his sisters as they regarded the slowly passing landscape. But when Freud came this way alone in 1913, it was the rattling, and not the beauty, that expressed his state of mind.

Freud cherished his summer holidays, which often reminded him of his early youth in Freiburg, Moravia (today Příbor in the Czech Republic). His father fared badly in business, and Freud's youth was spent in poverty. When he was three, the family left their Moravian home, eventually for urban Vienna, where he would spend almost the rest of his life. He did not see his birthplace again until he was sixteen; the visit prompted his earliest surviving letters, and ushered in a lifetime of writing. For Freud the Vienna woods were no substitute for the landscapes warm in his memory; in an essay written in 1899, when he was in his forties, Freud insisted that after leaving Freiburg, of his recollections, "nothing was worth remembering"—an astonishing comment from a psychoanalyst. Nearly every word from Freud's pen about Vienna betrays ambivalence. He once wrote his friend Wilhelm Fliess "But I am suffering from a bad case of spring fever, hungering for sunshine, flowers, a bit of blue water, just like a young man. I hate Vienna almost personally and, unlike the giant Antaeus, I gather fresh strength as soon as I lift my foot from hometown soil." Only at the end of his life, when, in repetition of childhood, he was forced into exile, would Freud express a more positive sentiment toward his lifelong home. "I still greatly loved the prison from which I have been released," he wrote sadly from London, where he had fled in exile after the Nazi occupation of Austria.

In sharp contrast to his pained affection for his actual home, Freud loved nature, and thrilled each summer in anticipation of his family's next country holiday, or mushroom hunting, strawberry picking, walking, and mountaineering. He declared that his intellect, too, took a holiday during these times, leaving him to revel in the mysterious splendor of nature, with its cycles of season and time, growth and decay—the ceaseless rhythmic symphony of life.

Every summer Freud delighted in the small things of nature and the precision of its workings. The flowers, mushrooms, rocks, and birds gripped his imagination more forcefully than the majesty of the sweeping views. Such overpowering sights left him speechless, or resorting to the well-worn descriptions of beloved poets he had long committed to memory. He preferred with his scientist's eye to catalogue the finite, to discern within the crystal patterns of the rock, or the flower's pistils, the armature of its satisfying structure.

Freud saw in nature the beauty and magic of the world, and nowhere more plainly than in the mushroom, whose pursuit he may have cherished even more than the fugitive mysteries of the mind. During his holidays he routinely scoured the mountains with his children in search of wild mushrooms. He was an expert in discerning which were edible, and which poisonous. In such moments, Martin Freud remembered, his father's ordered and buttoned-up exterior gave way to boyish exuberance. Anna Freud once told Lou Andreas-Salomé of the strict procedure her father prescribed. As Lou later recalled, "When they went collecting mushrooms he always told them to go into the wood quietly, and he still does this; there must be no chattering and they must roll up the bags they have brought under their arms, so that the mushrooms shall not notice. When their father found one he would cover it quickly with his hat, as though it were a butterfly. The little children—and now his grandchildren—used to believe what he said, while the bigger ones smiled at his credulity."

When, in writing *The Interpretation of Dreams,* Freud cast about for an analogy to describe the structure and shape of dreams, he found it in the mushroom's mycelia, the membranous fibers that weave together to form stalk and head, and that join together beneath the earth to connect them with others of their kind. A dream, like a mushroom, Freud thought, was an elaboration of its roots in the past, in the tumult of unconscious feelings that sustained and forced it into conscious awareness. And like a mushroom's subterranean tendrils, a dream's dense layers of meaning were fused and buried in the substratum of the dreamer's unconscious.

During these weeks, as every summer, Freud did not entirely abandon the busy social life he knew in Vienna. While in the Dolomites he received guests, including perhaps the writer Stefan Zweig, and enjoyed conversations with his landlord and fellow tourists, as well as the chance encounters of summer fellowship that were an expected pleasure of these holidays. Relieved of his busy schedule of patients and professional obligations, Freud also wrote letters, conducted the hectic business of his movement, and devoted time to writing. But in the summer of 1913, he wrote very little; his mind was elsewhere, on Munich, and the trouble brewing there. Toward the end of his stay in San Martino, he was visited by his analytic colleagues Sándor Ferenczi and Karl Abraham, with whom he spent long hours worrying how to handle the controversy awaiting them.

At the end of August, Freud left his family and traveled by carriage to Lake Garda, where, with Sándor Ferenczi, he boarded a train for Munich. He had reason to regret the end of his Italian idyll. He didn't enjoy train travel to begin with, and this train would convey him to the Fourth International Psychoanalytical Congress, to his showdown with Jung.

2

By 1913, more than a decade after the publication of *The Interpretation of Dreams* in 1899, Freud had emerged from the "splendid isolation" of his early years into prominence and notoriety, gathering about him a movement that already spanned continents. The previous year had seen his oldest children leave the family home, and a sense of emptiness grew at Berggasse 19, as the younger Freuds embarked on their own lives. By 1915, Freud rued time's recent advances: "One finds oneself suddenly old, when only a few years earlier one might still have considered oneself young."

The struggles of youth—the establishment of his profession, marriage, the death of his father, becoming a father himself, his self-analysis, and the creation of his masterpiece, *The Interpretation of Dreams*—lay behind him. Although he would live another quarter-century, Freud had begun to consider his life as drawing to an end; he thought of himself as belonging to the past, and looked toward death and departure, whose first stirrings had made themselves apparent in his own body, and which he saw mirrored in the natural world around him. But this was not the result of a new awareness brought on by the evidence of age: Freud had long known such feelings, and had felt his time to be short since he was a boy.

In *The Interpretation of Dreams,* Freud remembered his first glimpse of mortality. "When I was six years old and was given my first lessons by my mother, I was expected to believe that we were all made of earth and must therefore return to earth," and he refused to believe it. In illustration of this incredible statement, Freud's mother rubbed her hands together "just as she did in making dumplings, except there was no dough between them," and revealed to him the black, balled epidermis that came away in the friction. "My astonishment at this ocular demonstration knew no bounds," Freud wrote, "and I acquiesced in the belief which I was later to hear expressed in the words '*Du bist der Natur ein Tod schuldig*' [Thou owest Nature a death]."

The remark Freud borrowed, from *King Henry IV, Part I,* to express his youthful sentiment actually reads "Thou owest God a death." *God,* not *Nature.* The mistake (truly, a Freudian slip) gave pointed expression to Freud's atheism, and was striking testament to his preoccupation with the eventual disposition of the dead.

3

In a letter written on another summer holiday, a trip to Italy in September 1897, Freud confided to Wilhelm Fliess the goal of his travels: "to drink a punch made from Lethe." Freud revisited this allusion to classical mythology several times over the next years as he formulated his theory of the unconscious. The meaning was clear to anyone with a classical education at the time: In travel, Freud wanted to forget.

In Greek myth Lethe is the river of oblivion, from which the souls of the newly departed drink to forget the memories of their vanished lives, which torment their ghostly existence. In the next sentence of his letter to Fliess, Freud enlarged on what he intended with his metaphor, and what he sought in the forgetfulness of Italy: "Here and there I get a draft. One savors the strange kind of beauty and the enormous creative urge." Freud dreamt of restoring his creativity through exposure to Italy's beauty.

When Freud wrote this letter, he was embarking on the most intensely creative period of his life—the years of his self-analysis, which he had begun only months earlier, and which would culminate in *The Interpretation of Dreams,* through which he would introduce psychoanalysis to the world. He did not elaborate further in this letter what he meant, and what he did say is puzzling, for it suggests that the road to creativity lies, paradoxically, in forgetting—especially in the forgetting inspired by the experience of beauty.

Freud's meaning grows even more obscure in light of another letter to Fliess, written three months later, in anticipation of their reunion. "It will be so invigorating for me to chat with you, without a care and seriously, after I have for months again harbored the most *meschugge* matters in my head, without emptying it, and otherwise do not have a sensible person to speak to. Once again, a draft of punch made of Lethe."

Meschugge, a Yiddish word used colloquially to denote nonsense or crazy thinking, derives from the ancient Hebrew for "wandering," as the Jews did upon their exile from Egypt—and as Ulysses did for the decade of the *Odyssey*—in search of the home they had lost. In this second letter, then, Freud expressed his longing for the distraction of his friend's company, to clear his head of thoughts that would not give him peace, so that he might return to vital work. Yet here his inspiration seems to require not forgetting but homecoming—rest.

The amnesiac ghosts of the underworld would later surface in *The Interpretation of Dreams*, where Freud compared the recollections of the dead to the immortality of unconscious memories. In the unconscious, memories can never be forgotten and are never lost. "If I may use a simile, they are only capable of annihilation in the same sense as the ghosts in the underworld of the *Odyssey*—ghosts which awoke to new life as soon as they tasted blood."

In the passage of the *Odyssey* to which Freud refers, Ulysses, in order to learn his destiny, ventures into the underworld; there, by bringing the blood of the living to the dead, he causes them to remember and to recount to him their lives. In Freud's analogy, unconscious memories—repressed, forgotten, and therefore forgotten by the world—and the feelings attached to them are revived when they are attached to some new life experience, which excites the old impulse; they transfer their energy to the new currents (as, for instance, when one becomes violently angry over a trivial matter). They are thus enlivened, Freud says, like the dead who drink the blood of the living, and remember the lives they longed to forget.

Freud used this analogy in the important section of *The Interpretation of Dreams* where he explains the concept of "repression"—the idea that memories remain buried in our minds forever—and testifies to the double-edged nature of such memories. These memories, the ghosts of the unconscious, are as paradoxical as the ghosts of myth: outside awareness, they haunt human activity with a kind of negative remembrance, by their very absence. Brought to the surface through indirection, by a fit of inexplicable rage or sorrow, or by a particularly vivid recollection, forgotten or repressed memories are enlivened in us, without our knowing about them, except through our feelings and what they make us do. Freud's allusions to the contrasting drinking habits of the dead—from the waters of oblivion and the blood of remembrance—further emphasized the importance he attached to the fate of the dead in the memory of the living, and to the vital role played by the past in the shaping of unconscious memory itself.

In 1913, in his book *Daniel*, the philosopher and theologian Martin Buber suggested a knotty metaphor for artistic inspiration: In order to create, poets drink both from the river Lethe and from a river of remembrance. Buber meant to underscore the difficulty of the poetic enterprise: to take memory and make it new—to take the forgotten dead of the past and bring them to life again, through memory. While he meant his statement as an indication of how man related, in creativity, to God, Buber's formulation recalls Freud's difficult metaphors. It was, perhaps, even closer to Freud's own experience.

The river of the underworld and its forgetful dead were described in the *Odyssey,* a book that meant a great deal to Freud. In the passage he referred to in *The Interpretation of Dreams,* where Ulysses ventures into the underworld in order to find his way back home, he meets the shades of those whom he knew in life, including the heroes Achilles, Hector, and Ajax, and others fallen at Troy, and discovers that his rivals are rivals no longer in death. Further along, Ulysses weeps guiltily at the sight of his father, Laertes, who had died during his long absence. Finally he meets the blind prophet Teiresias, from whom he learns the shape of his fate: He will return home to grow old prosperously; at the end of his life he must leave home again; he will die at the mercy of the ocean—whose divinity, Poseidon, he has offended by killing his son the Cyclops—but he will die peacefully, and nobly.

Ulysses struck many in Freud's era as a very modern figure: an exile (as Freud himself would one day become), an overthrown king, a man living outside contemporary time, marooned and passing from one isolated world to the next, overwhelmed by nostalgia, by the desire to return home. In an era of sweeping political and economic change, as the Europe that Freud and his contemporaries knew seemed to be disappearing, Ulysses could represent those who yearned to turn away from the uncertainty and "decadence" of contemporary Europe, toward an imaginary past resembling their nostalgic memories.

Faced with the choice of living with the nymph Calypso on her island paradise or returning to Ithaca, the hardscrabble island of which he is king, Ulysses chooses to go home, and the epic chronicles his struggle to do so against determined (in fact, divine) opposition. His choice must have appealed to Freud, for it resembles the hard choice posed by the analytic enterprise: to remain in the world of fantasy, pleasing and unreal, or to forge one's destiny in the hard school of the world, in the face of certain disappointment, suffering, and mortality.

Like Ulysses exiled from the happy land of his childhood, Freud said he was never happy in Vienna, where he nevertheless spent most of his life. The parallel was greater than Freud knew, as the elements of Teiresias's prophecy for the hero's last destiny—great age, a second exile, and a seemingly retributive but ultimately noble death—would also characterize Freud's own ending.

4

Not far from San Martino di Castrozza, at nearly 3,800 feet above sea level, lies the mountain village of Lavarone. The winters come early and linger, but in all seasons it is spectacular, offering panoramic views of the mountains and valleys of the Alps to the west and the Adriatic Sea to the east.

It was in rustic Lavarone that Freud, who opposed many technological innovations, including radio and telephone, skeptically climbed into an automobile for the first time. It was here, too, that Freud first brought his family to vacation in the Dolomites, and they returned for each of three seasons (there is still a plaque outside the Hotel Du Lac commemorating Freud's presence there). In his son Martin's memoir of family holidays, Lavarone stands out most in their summer travels.

Martin repeats the story, told by one of his sisters, of how Freud came to Lavarone. Freud's brother Alexander had, years earlier in Vienna, befriended "a gifted poet but not successful in a pecuniary sense," who, like the Freuds, came from Bohemia. Through Alexander, Freud became acquainted with the poet; he later took Anna to visit the unfortunate man on his deathbed. As they parted, the dying poet expressed to his visitors his wish to see the laburnum blossom in Lavarone once more. Sometime afterward, hiking in the Dolomites while scouting a summer retreat for his family, Freud recalled the dying man's wish, and went to the place himself, even staying in the same Hotel Du Lac, which the poet had remembered.

The laburnum is a tree with a brilliant yellow flower, beautiful but poisonous. It is a spring flower native to the region where Freud was born. In Lavarone, laburnum blooms late; the eye finds in those high mountains sights and plants and colors that have already had their time in the valleys below.

In his writings, Freud never mentions the mysterious dying poet who led him to Lavarone, and his identity remains unknown. Martin Freud's account, derived from his sister's recollection, may not be reliable; in any case, he himself disliked the story, calling it "a little too sentimental" for his taste.

It *is* sentimental. The anecdote involves a pilgrimage made in memory of a dead man. It is, in this sense, a journey to the land of the dead.

5

Barely two years after Freud's 1913 visit to San Martino di Castrozza, the mountains surrounding the peaceful town rang with gunfire, their ancient faces terraced with soldiers' trenches, pierced and shattered and burned by the efficient artillery of modern warfare. From a similar mountain on the Eastern Front, Martin Freud would be shot at and shelled; in a letter, his father told him he hoped that he would himself shoot back not a little. All around its borders, the mountains of the Austro-Hungarian Empire were turned into forges of violence. Then the shooting stopped, and silence overtook the mountains again. Eventually the retreating Austrian forces, beaten back beyond the mountains by their adversaries, left behind—among the bodies, walls, and scars of rock—the remnants of their imperial legacy, and the ineradicable roots of their culture, which had grown there. Hapsburg rule of the Dolomites soon ceased, the former governors fated to return only as tourists, and their presence to persist only in the living memory of the language and the legends that lingered in their wake.

CHAPTER FOUR

Freud was a talented student of languages; besides his native German, he learned Spanish, French, Latin, Greek, English, and Italian. He especially admired English, the adopted tongue of his two older half brothers, who left Freiburg for Manchester, England, while Freud was still a child.

One of his sisters told the story that as an adolescent Freud loved the Gettysburg Address. Moved by its eloquent sentiment, the aspiring Englishman and orator memorized the text in its original language, and recited it often before an indulgent family audience. One can only surmise the joy he felt as he mouthed the words, in that strange, wonderful tongue, thrilled by the grace, precision, and lofty power of its cadence. He might have almost believed himself president of the United States, standing humbly on a field of grief.

Throughout his life, Freud was renowned for his astounding memory. Martin Freud recalled an evening from his own childhood when his father asked him to recite the opening of the *Iliad* in Greek. When his recollection faltered, his father took up the recitation, although he had not seen the Greek text in more than forty years.

Freud was raised in an age that prized memory and relied on it, and in which it was both a cultural and a personal virtue to remember. It was a time that celebrated both classicism and Romanticism, an era whose literature and arts had, as in the Renaissance, taken the past as their model, and so moved forward by looking back. In German-speaking countries in particular, the flowering during the eighteenth and nineteenth centuries of a native literature brought with it a renewed reverence for the ancient cultures that preceded it, and to which, in search of its past, it traced its lineage. In the Gymnasiums, students read deeply in the literature of the past, and learned the languages and works above all of Greek and Latin writers. Raised in this tradition, Freud admired these classical ancestors throughout his life, and within his head dwelt the worlds of their literatures.

The Gymnasium education in which the young Freud was steeped was modeled on a vision of humanism, first articulated by such figures as the polymath Alexander von Humboldt (whose writings included the multivolume *Kosmos*, which purported to describe all the known phenomena in the universe). This vision held man to be the center of a universe he revered, his task to unravel its mysteries. These mysteries—the phenomena of the natural world—were held sacred, as was the human mission of their comprehension. It was through this knowledge that *Homo sapiens sapiens*—man who knows he knows—would fulfill his destiny and play his part in the larger orders of nature. An intrinsic part of this knowledge was a sense of the history, cultures, and languages of the past on which the present was founded.

Memorization of the kind Freud was used to, no longer favored by educators, is a way of taking words into oneself. We often hear of writers who, to better understand the process of composition, copy over the writings of those they admire, and so relive in effigy the writer's effort. In so doing, they hope to relive the works' creation by retracing its language, using the words as a blueprint to the impulses that engendered them. In an age in which the names of Homer, Plato, Shakespeare, and Goethe were esteemed as signposts of human culture, knowledge of their works was transmitted, in the first place, by memorization, as a way of forcing the Gymnasium student to take the particular writer's words into himself, and make them his own.

Before writing came into common use (barely three centuries ago even in much of the "civilized" Western world), people relied on memory to preserve the products of the human intellect. Earlier still, the epics of Homer were handed down orally for centuries, before a recording system—writing—was devised that no longer depended on living memory. In the process, those stories were modified, evolving to meet the needs of their successive audiences. In this way, old stories were renewed, and the vibrant past resurrected in the present. Taking his cue from these lessons of oral history, Freud would come to understand the psyche as an instrument for both caring for and containing the past, and for reconciling it to the present.

Even as a youngster declaiming Lincoln's potent, graceful eulogy for the thousands of men fallen upon a Pennsylvania field, Freud seems to have sensed the power of inspiration that dwelt in memories of loss. But he could not then have anticipated how far his inquiries into memory would take him, or what they would reveal to him of his own history.

2

Forsan et haec olim meminisse juvabit.
Someday, perhaps it will be a joy to
remember even these things.

— VERGIL, *AENEID*, I, 203
(quoted in Freud's "Screen Memories")

In the summer of 1872, sixteen-year-old Sigismund Freud (he would soon change his name to the more heroic Sigmund) returned to his Moravian birthplace, which his family had left when he was three. The occasion for the departure had been traumatic for the family; Freud's father, a wool merchant, had lost his business when the industry collapsed. The family was forced to move, first to Leipzig and then to Vienna, and never regained the measure of prosperity it had enjoyed in the country.

Freud would later recall this upheaval as the end of his idyllic childhood, after which "it seems to me, nothing is worth remembering." Unlike later recollections, Freud's early memories remained with him his whole life, vivid and vibrant: memories of his play in Freiburg's fields; of an injury sustained while ransacking a cupboard; of his nursemaid's stories of the Bible, and her ministrations. Through thirteen years of absence, these early, almost incoherent memories sustained him in his new, unloved residence.

How momentous, then, his homecoming must have seemed. Its impact may be seen in his letters from the period, the earliest that survive. The Freiburg visit is the first time that we know Freud from his own pen—the sojourn is the opening chapter in the future analyst's long career of autobiography.

It was a summer of renewed friendships with boyhood pals Emil Fluss and Eduard Silberstein, of lazy mornings and long afternoon rambles in the familiar countryside. It was also the summer that Sigmund felt the initial pull of adolescent sexual attraction. Freud's first known correspondence, with his friend Silberstein after the journey to Freiburg, is filled with puzzling references to "Ich." This was the abbreviation for Ichthyosaura, a fishlike, reptilian female dinosaur from the Saurian epoch, and the subject of a poem by the contemporary popular humorist Josef Viktor von Scheffel. The poem is narrated by a jealous male Ichthyosaurus, who deplores the corrupt state of his prehistoric world and, above all, the licentiousness of one "Iguanodon, the rapscallion, / No pleasures he ever resists, /

For e'en in the broadest of daylight / The Ichthyosaura he kissed." In apparent consequence of this treachery, the world of the dinosaurs perishes.

In their first playful letters, the two friends appear to describe any one of the local girls who caught their shy boyish fancy as an unchaste "Ichthyosaura," or else as a "principle" (another of the euphemisms they employed to denote an object of affection). But soon there could be little doubt that the reptile in question in Freud's furtive letters was one girl in particular: Gisela Fluss.

Not quite twelve, Gisela was the eldest daughter of the Fluss family, with whom the Freuds had a close friendship of long standing; Freud stayed with them during his holiday in Moravia. On the surface, the relationship did not amount to much. Gisela, herself at home on holiday, was in Freiburg for little more than a week of Freud's visit, before returning to school in Breslau; during that interval the outward relation between Freud and his beloved did not go beyond respectful acquaintance. "The affection appeared to me like a beautiful spring day, and only the nonsensical Hamlet in me, my diffidence, stood in the way of my finding it a refreshing pleasure to converse with the half-naive, half-cultured young lady." The young lover was overwhelmed in his dealings with the girl by adolescent shyness and, as far as we know, never told Gisela of his feelings.

From Freud's letters, however, one gets a clear idea of his passion. "Gisela's beauty is wild, I might say Thracian," he writes, and he sounds positively Petrarchan as he celebrates her "aquiline nose . . . long black hair and . . . firm lips." When his friend Eduard Silberstein has the opportunity to dance with her, one can nearly feel Freud's pen tremble: "You will have the pleasure, which cannot be expressed in words, or only feebly or inadequately[,] of 'touching' Gisela"—something, he adds, that he has "less motivation and occasion to do."

From the beginning of his infatuation, Freud struggled to master the feelings that Gisela provoked in him. "I have soothed all my turbulent thoughts and only flinch slightly when her mother mentions Gisela's name at table," he noted at one point, evidently proud of his self-control. He rather implausibly (but for the future psychoanalyst perhaps prophetically) attributed the cause of his passion to an admiration for the little girl's mother, in whom Freud found an enviable combination of education and enlightened attitudes. In any case, the choicest outpourings of lyrical expression, as well as the mocking monikers, were reserved for Gisela.

It is not known whether Freud's feelings for Gisela persisted with similar intensity over the next three years, or whether they receded for a time, as mention of her became sparse in his letters. But in the fall of 1875, three years after the first flowering of Freud's affection, he received the terrible news of Gisela's engagement. Sigmund conveyed the tidings to Eduard in the form of a lengthy verse: "You can imagine that only a most extraordinary occasion could have inspired me to such poetic heights." The poem is a *Hochzeitscarmen*, traditionally written in celebration of nuptials. He begins in imitation of

Homer, with an invocation of the Muse, but it quickly becomes apparent that his subject is a more current concern.

"Sing me, oh Muse[,] the praises of Ichthyosaura communis / . . . To the Academía so bright an example / . . . Yet she crushed the Chalk that ensued in her wake, / Until this too turned to dust—for nothing on earth is eternal." The poem continues in praise of Ichthyosaura's physical beauty, although the casual reader may be forgiven for thinking that she comes off rather badly. "Not too large was her stature . . . / Spherical she appeared and gloriously rounded, / Rounded her face . . . / Rounded her girth, and if the poet be free / To probe with a curious eye what is normally hidden from view, / He will find the sphere's principle pervading the forms / Blessed night reveals to the fortunate groom."

Cleverness and bawd give way to the poet's more pronounced ambivalence in the succeeding passages, as the spurned lover vents to his frustration. "But of *one* qualm relieve me, oh Muse, for large it does loom. / . . . That the spirit but dully moves in the sunny flesh, / That reason's sway in the tiny brain is but frail, / And confined by the ribbons, the bows, and the plaits, / That the eye was not pierced by learning's sharp rays."

And in an instant, Freud's love is crushed, like the chalk pounded to dust by his beloved's dinosaur alter ego. Gisela's beauty is erased in the poet's estimation by her supposed poverty of intellect, by the torpor of her domestic destiny, and the presumed banality of wedded bliss. The poem's last lines show the young cuckold at his cruelest: "May blessings abound in their house . . . / And so may they both live out their allotted span, / Like the insects and worms that inhabit the earth, / Blesséd with splendid digestion and lungs, / Never plagued by the *spirit*, such is the *Academía's* wish." Stinging from her indifference to his own passionate "spirit," the poet bitterly wishes her a long, loveless marriage.

One is struck by the alacrity with which Freud's fondness has curdled, how changed is this poetic expression of disillusionment by an impersonal "Academía" (an imaginary society of which Freud was the sole member) from his assurance that "for the moment . . . I do not suffer any conflict between ideal and reality, and . . . I am incapable of making fun of Gisela." But as a much older Freud would assure us, this leap is not so great after all: every emotion contains its opposite—hate joined, ab ovo, with the love it despises. And indeed, by a real miracle of history, there exists another document, an earlier draft of Freud's epithalamium, that casts the sorrows of young Sigmund in a very different light.

Gone are the classical pretensions, the mocking Saurian epithets by which Freud distanced himself from his feelings, replaced by frank expression of the pangs of despised love. "To put into German words [the] wretched, abominable despair, your letter so suddenly cast into the depths of the heart— / . . . Woe is me, woe; I rage, pain sears my breast. / Scarce can I grasp the abominable fate." The poet then considers the course taken by his fictive Romantic ancestor, Goethe's hero Werther. "Send me forthwith two potassium cyanides, two green ones, / five drops of ether, / . . . plant of hemlock . . . / Arsenic, all white and pure, send me today. / Provide me with a sharp razor, / a revolver, lead bullets with shot." Reading this, one fears for the young man's life—though it is hard not to admire his command of the varieties of self-slaughter.

The poem betrays the influence of German Romanticism on the author. The young writer's fictional, poetic rejoinder of suicide to disappointment in love is that of Goethe's Werther and that dreamt of by Hamlet, twin icons of the Romantic Sturm und Drang sentiment prevalent during Freud's youth.

This is not to say that the feelings expressed in Freud's poem were not genuine; on the contrary, we should take them as a faithful portrait of the young man's anguish, rendered in the idiom and according to the literary conventions of the time. Yet he discarded this first draft, evidently already subjecting himself in youth to the relentless self-criticism to which he would submit all his later writing.

Looking again at the later poem, one senses that in passing from the first version to the second, Freud has rejected the sentimental feeling that left him vulnerable to the pain of heartache and, with it, the aesthetic zeitgeist of his time, by which, on the evidence of these early letters and his later work, he was profoundly influenced. Between the first version and the second, the emphasis shifts from the poet's subjective, private feeling of loss, to the substitutive expression of that loss by its conversion into anger and spite, into wicked caricature and witty disdain.

The poet of the first version, a Romantic, might be characterized as suffering from what Freud later termed melancholia, the pathological form of mourning. The poet of the second version, in contrast, is tormented by what Freud had described in "On Transience" as a rebellion in the mind against mourning— a refusal by the bereaved to acknowledge the pain of loss, which results in a sort of paralysis of the libido or affection once directed toward the loved one, a refusal much like that of which Freud accused his companions in "On Transience."

At the conclusion of the letter accompanying the bitter second version of the *Hochzeitscarmen*, the grieving hero abandons his earlier Romantic sentiments altogether and makes a final-sounding pronouncement:

> *Herewith the Formation [his infatuation for Gisela] comes to an end. I now bury the magic wand that aided her education, and may a new age begin without forces working in secret, that has no need of poetry and fantasy. Let no one seek a principle save in the present, not in the alluvium or diluvium, nowhere save among the children of man, not in the gruesome primeval past where wild creatures could consume oxygen of the atmosphere punished by man.*

No more will Freud indulge in the follies of childhood; echoing Shakespeare's reticent wizard Prospero, he buries the wand of imaginative power and commits himself to a future without fantasy, without poetry. No more will he seek fulfillment in the past or in the imagination; he will turn himself to the present, to the study of a reality that, when approached with objectivity and rigor, would offer up even its most obscure and irrational ways to clear understanding. Shortly after this unhappy affair, Sigmund announced his decision to become a natural scientist.

3

In 1899, some twenty-five years after the Gisela episode, Freud published an essay titled "Screen Memories," about early childhood recollection. At the time, he was proud of what he had done; as he wrote his friend Wilhelm Fliess, "While producing it, I liked it immensely—which does not augur well for its future fate."

In the essay, Freud relates a conversation between himself and a patient, "a thirty-eight-year-old man of university education." The man can make no sense of his own earliest memory, and asks Freud to help him puzzle it out. He tells Freud:

> *I see a rectangular, rather steeply sloping piece of meadow-land, green and thickly grown, in the green there are a great number of yellow flowers—evidently common dandelions. At the top end of the meadow there is a cottage and in front of the cottage door two women are standing chatting busily, a peasant-woman with a handkerchief on her head and a children's nurse. Three children are playing in the grass. One of them is myself (between the ages of two and three); the two others are my boy cousin, who is a year older than [I], and his sister, who is almost exactly the same age as I am. We are picking the yellow flowers and each of us is holding a bunch*

of flowers we have already picked. The little girl has the best bunch; and, as though by mutual agreement, we—the two boys—fall on her and snatch away her flowers. She runs up the meadow in tears and as a consolation the peasant-woman gives her a big piece of black bread. Hardly have we seen this than we throw the flowers away, hurry to the cottage and ask to be given some bread too. And we are in fact given some; the peasant-woman cuts the loaf with a long knife. In my memory the bread tastes quite delicious—and at that point the scene breaks off.

The patient adds that it is the yellow of the flowers and the taste of the bread that are most prominent in his recollection. He cannot remember clearly when the events in the memory could have taken place, and is confounded that he should remember this insignificant moment out of all that happened during his first years, which were in fact very eventful.

Freud asks his patient whether he can recall when he first became aware of the memory. The patient thinks for a moment, and is surprised to remember quite precisely, that it came to him as an adolescent on holiday, visiting for the first time the rural town where he was born:

Those holidays, when I was seventeen, were my first holidays in the country, and, as I have said, I stayed with a family with whom we were friends and who had risen greatly in the world since our move. I could compare the comfort reigning there with our own style of living at home in the town. But it is no use evading the subject any longer: I must admit that there was something else that excited me powerfully. I was seventeen, and in the family where I was staying there was a daughter of fifteen, with whom I immediately fell in love. It was my first calf-love and sufficiently intense, but I kept it completely secret. After a few days the girl went off to her school (from which she too was home for the holidays) and it was this separation after such a short acquaintance that brought my longings to a really high pitch. I passed many hours in solitary walks through the lovely woods that I had found once more and spent my time building castles in the air. These, strangely enough, were not concerned with the future but sought to improve upon the past. . . . I had not the slightest doubt, of course, that in the circumstances created by my imagination I should have loved her just as passionately as I really seemed to then. A strange thing. For when I see her now from time to time—she happens to have married someone here—she is quite exceptionally indifferent to me. Yet I can remember quite well for what a long time afterwards I was affected by the yellow color of the dress she was wearing when we first met, whenever I saw the same color anywhere else.

With this fresh information in hand, Freud felt ready to reconstruct the significance of the patient's memory. The scene, he said, was in fact the expression of the patient's wishes and fantasies, or rather, those fantasies and wishes that belonged to the patient's adolescence. In the intense yellow of the flowers, the analyst saw the reprisal of the yellow dress of the young man's beloved. In the exquisite piquancy of the bread, the memory of whose flavor still excited the patient's appetite, he discerned the sweet taste the patient's life in the country would have held for him, had he only remained in his childhood home, and not followed his actual course in moving to the city and going off to school, a "slave to his books," struggling to "earn his bread."

Even more, in the image of the flowers snatched from the little girl, Freud found his patient's truest wish, proscribed by propriety and cast out into the obscurity of childhood. For in the stealing of the girl's flowers (by which she is "deflowered"), Freud finds an allusion to the patient's desire, not for the girl of the memory, but for the later girl, the girl of the summer holiday and the patient's youthful love.

Freud believed that the memory's power and vividness in the patient's mind derived not from his childhood or from the events recalled, but from the later experience of his adolescence. The youth's wishes, which because of their forbidden nature could not be consciously acknowledged, found their expression in the harmless childhood memory; behind the bright colors and the wonderful flavor lurked desire and regret.

When the patient heard Freud's interpretation, he resisted it; he doubted the authenticity of his original memory, suggesting it to be a figment of his imagination, conjured up to represent his secret, unconscious wishes. But Freud defended the memory as genuine; the patient's mind had not imagined new memories, creating out of whole cloth a new past for him. Instead, it had chosen from the patient's old memories those that served its purpose, and refashioned them in order to express forbidden wishes.

4

The patient Freud described in this vignette was none other than Freud himself, and the holiday described was his own return to Freiburg; the young man (like the flower-picking toddler) was his younger self, and the girl in the yellow dress, Gisela Fluss. "Screen Memories" is the first of a long line of publications in which the reader beholds the spectacle of Sigmund Freud, the proper bourgeois doctor, having a conversation with himself in public about his most private thoughts. Reading it with this knowledge, the essay takes on a new poignancy, and added meaning.

As a psychoanalyst, Freud believed that people revise their own history through memory, and very likely don't know it. Our memories, he maintained, are not the faithful archives we'd like to think they are, reproducing in detail the events of our lives as they happen. Nor are they like photographs that we frame and snap of our own volition. Our minds manipulate our recollections, to tell us things about ourselves we don't otherwise know, and can't know, because they are painful, or dangerous, or at odds with other important ideas we have about ourselves.

Freud believed his memory of the scene on the hill, first recalled during his adolescent homecoming, was the disguised
expression of his young feelings for Gisela Fluss. The yellow of
the flowers evoked the yellow dress he remembered her wearing; the bread, the sweet taste of the country life he was denied.
But by displacing the memory backward in time, to the innocent age of his childhood, the painful feelings of desire and its
disappointment were experienced without the unbearable recollection of the painful event itself.

According to Freud's theory, the universal difficulty in re-
calling the events of earliest childhood is the result of an amne-
sia brought on by repression, the legacy of the turmoil into
which each child's instinctual life is cast during the first years of
life, and especially by the advent and overthrow of the love associated with the Oedipus complex. What memories do linger,
Freud tells us, are of a very pointed sort, freighted with feelings
from the hidden past of infancy, and from events in the child's
later life that revive them. For Freud the past is alive in the present; but the present also revives the past, breathes life into the
old embers with each new breath.

What Freud remembered most vividly from his first memory of life were its sensory elements, the brilliance of yellow
wildflowers and the flavor of bread. The realm of the senses im-
pinges powerfully on our memories, though in describing and
thinking about sensory experiences we are often reduced to
barren images and clichéd phrases, confronted with the poverty
of language to depict them. For Freud, so much of our feeling

life takes refuge in the senses precisely because of the gap between our ability to perceive these things and our ability to represent them to ourselves. In these dark places in our perception—the inarticulate perception of odor or color, the blurred part of the image, the uncertainly remembered phrase from the dream—forbidden feelings conceal themselves to avoid expulsion or expression, existing instead like a kind of shadow government, manipulating their owner by cryptic signals from secret hiding places. When listening to a patient, Freud would watch for inconsistencies and exaggerations, or "bagatelles," in the narrative, for places where the story didn't work, made no sense, and burrowed further there.

Freud did not begin to comprehend the close connection between memory and desire until undertaking his own self-analysis, which resulted in "Screen Memories" and, soon after, the invention of psychoanalysis. But he had already found in himself the basic elements for this discovery as a brokenhearted teenager, whose heartache was so painful that he thought to kill himself, and then, in a wild change of heart, vilified the tender object of his affection with great cruelty, burying under his scorn the love that had so hurt him. He had, in effect, rewritten the history of his heart, very consciously and even methodically (in hexameter!), much the same way that, a quarter-century later, an older Freud would say we all unconsciously rewrite our heart's histories, by how we remember those histories—by fusing the reality of the past with the fantasies, wishes, and regrets that were the secret sharers of our experience, in ways that make our memories truer than the experiences from which they are derived.

In later years, when he had become famous, Freud was reluctant to have "Screen Memories" reproduced; most readers became aware of it only when the first comprehensive collection of his works was published, a few years before his death; even then, he initially refused to allow its inclusion, though he later relented. With the publication, in late 1899, of *The Interpretation of Dreams,* which is filled with autobiographical information, even a casual reader would have been able to identify the patient as Freud himself. That Freud was so bashful about the episode described in "Screen Memories," when he was astonishingly open about other areas of his life (sexual desire for his mother! murderous wishes against his father!), is some indication of the personal importance he apparently attached to the Gisela episode. In all subsequent references to his childhood love for her, Freud treats it as an event of little consequence. It may be that these comments reflect his true feelings, or at least the feelings of the Freud who had grown up far from the country, become a doctor, founded a new branch of science, and married and started a family. But behind that successful older man looms the shadow of a younger one—who poured out his heart in a poem of frustrated devotion, then renounced that same love, and with it all poetic inspiration, then buried it in an ostensibly inconsequential memory of childhood, where it would be rediscovered years later, like a time capsule, by his older self, who could scarcely believe the strength of his own early passion, but who was able, nonetheless, to take great pleasure in writing it down, and once again making it his own.

5

Freud's vengeful wedding poem was not the only creative product of his youth. During the tumultuous years of adolescence he was nearly as prolific a writer as he was as an adult. The list of his works leading up to the epithalamium (compiled by the author himself in a letter to Eduard Silberstein) includes imaginary histories, stories, sonnets, and translations of fanciful, spurious works. With the poem that bore witness to his early disappointment in love, young Freud renounced poetry for the certainty of science. But he could not disown his memories, or the impulse to understand the past they concealed. In his psychoanalytic work, he constantly refined his own history, returning time and again to the experiences of his past in order to create them anew, to expose them to new lights and different kinds of observation.

From his own experience Freud learned that life's events, whether dramatic or humdrum, often steal unnoticed into perception, are stored up within recollection, and over time take on successive meanings as they are joined with others, seemingly unrelated, all worked into an endlessly rewoven tapestry. This experience of the everyday artistry of memory imbued in him, despite (or because of) his disavowal of poetry, an awe of intuitive creation. Art became for Freud the limit of his knowledge, before which his psychoanalytic, "scientific" understanding was made to lay down its arms. As he wrote in 1913 in *Totem and Taboo*:

> *In only a single field of our civilization has the omnipotence of thoughts been retained, and that is in the field of art. Only in art does it still happen that a man who is consumed by desires performs something resembling the accomplishment of those desires and that what he does in play produces emotional effects—thanks to artistic illusion—just as though it were something real.*

So the adolescent Freud turned his energies to science, and professed himself closed to the palpable, sensual pleasures of art, sensible only of art's appeal to the intellect. But the truth was not so simple. In psychoanalysis Freud would combine, confuse, and redraw the boundary between art and life, finding again and again in his own remembrances and those of his patients new "screen memories"—unconscious fictions that, like his childhood recollection of a yellow hilltop, were portals to a kaleidoscopic past of infinite richness and ambiguity, each memory containing the core, kernel, and secret of the dreamer's soul and desire, and the history of what had been loved, and what lost.

In the margins of such a memory one might trace out an image of a person's whole life, his preoccupations, what drove him to rage and what made him grieve, and in so doing give voice to the very passions that inspire art, which (as Freud once wrote of Gustave Flaubert's *The Temptation of Saint Anthony*)

in the most condensed fashion and with unsurpassable vivid-ness throws at one's head the whole trashy world: for it calls up not only the great problems of knowledge, but the real riddles of life, all the conflicts of feelings and impulses, and it confirms the awareness of our perplexity in the mysterious-ness that reigns everywhere. These questions, it is true, are al-ways there, and one should always be thinking of them. What one does, however, is to confine oneself to a narrow aim every hour and every day and one gets used to the idea that to con-cern oneself with these enigmas is the task of a special hour, in the belief that they exist only in these special hours. Then they suddenly assail one in the morning and rob one of one's com-posure and one's spirits.

CHAPTER FIVE

Psycho-analysis . . . can thus demonstrate new connecting threads in the "weaver's masterpiece" spread between the instinctual endowments, the experiences and the works of an artist.

—FROM FREUD'S GOETHE PRIZE ADDRESS

I n 1930, Freud received the Goethe Prize, Germany's highest literary award, bestowed by the city of Frankfurt on "a personality of established achievement whose creative work is worthy of an honour dedicated to Goethe's memory." It was the greatest public recognition he would receive for his work, but it was given not in consideration of his scientific achievements but for his gifts as a writer.

In his acceptance speech, Freud compared the prize's namesake with another creative genius. "In Leonardo's nature the scientist did not harmonize with the artist, he interfered with him and perhaps in the end stifled him. In Goethe's life both personalities found room side by side: at different times each allowed the other to predominate."

Freud's ardent but unsuccessful pursuit of official recognition, above all through a Nobel Prize (which already then carried with it global prestige), was dogged by the same problem faced by Leonardo da Vinci and Goethe, a problem that stood near the heart of Freud's entire enterprise: Whether to regard his work as science or literature.

What is psychoanalysis? Is it art or science? Despite Freud's insistence that he was a scientist—and that he lacked poetic imagination—his statements on the matter, as well as the puzzling nature of psychoanalysis, suggest a more complicated picture.

In an essay on creative writers, Freud called them irresponsible toward Truth, the pursuit of which he regarded as the essential characteristic of scientific work and of psychoanalysis. Seeking only emotional effect, the artist was free to build his story or painting from anything at his disposal, real or imagined, true or false. The artist was, that is, the antithesis of the scientist, whose scope of inquiry was bound by the world around him, as it was and as he could see it.

Psychoanalysis, however, does not fit easily into the phyla of science. Frequently, Freud compared analytic investigation to physics; both sought to explain phenomena that could not be directly observed, but must be inferred, guessed at, like the effect of black holes on gravity. Simple truths are hard to come by in the study of black holes—a term that, after all, is only a figure of speech, a metaphor, to describe something beyond perception—and even more so in the analyst's exploration of an individual's psychology, with all its exaggerations and associations and *feelings*. The analyst's areas of inquiry—the elusive feelings and motive forces of human beings—had historically been the subjects of literature, philosophy, and art. Was not analysis, then, just a new mode of literature, and Freud's work more akin to the complex moral fictions of Dostoyevsky and Shakespeare than to the objective, revealed truths of Newton, Darwin, or Einstein?

In the scientific climate in which Freud's work emerged, these questions mattered. The charge that psychoanalysis was unscientific was often leveled in order to challenge its use in the treatment of mental illness. Depression, obsession, mania, hysteria, and other such illnesses were then (as now) widely regarded as primarily physiological in origin, the result of organic degeneration or defect. Artists, meanwhile, were quick to claim Freud for their own, and in literary experiments such as the automatic writing of the Surrealists (in which writers scribbled away without regard to the meaning of what they wrote, or even whether they were forming intelligible sentences), they emulated —improperly, in Freud's view—psychoanalytic methods.

At the same time that Freud questioned artists' commitment to "Truth," he considered their creativity the highest human achievement, and that most shrouded in mystery. Psychoanalysis, which had offered explanations for everything from religion to war to love, was mute before art. Freud's reluctance to "analyze" the artistic process (though he did not hesitate to investigate the lives of individual artists, for clues to the conflicts he thought were expressed in their works) was due in large part to his personal admiration for the great artists of Western history—Shakespeare, Goethe, Leonardo, Michelangelo. He considered psychoanalysis, and all science, to be fundamentally indebted to such artists, who, in their creative works, seemed to him to "know through intuition—or rather from a delicate self-observation—everything that I have discovered by laborious work in other people."

By his own account, Freud's choice of a career in science, over law or poetry, was inspired by his reading in the Gymnasium a popular essay ascribed to Goethe titled "Nature." (Although it was attributed to Goethe at the time Freud was in school and was written very much in his style, it was actually by Georg Christoph Tobler, a Swiss theologian who had known Goethe.) In the essay, Nature is characterized as a loving, all-embracing essence, from which proceed the fruits of knowledge, labor, and love. At first blush, the language and ideas of the essay resemble those Freud would express in "On Transience." "She [Nature] brings forth ever new forms: what is there, never was; what was, never will return. All is new, and yet forever old. . . . All her effort seems bent toward individuality, and she cares nothing for individuals. She builds always, destroys always, and her workshop is beyond our reach." Later, the words seem to herald the great theme of psychoanalysis, the battle between the instincts toward love and aggression: "[Nature's] crown is love. Only through love do we come to her. She opens chasms between all beings, and each seeks to devour the other. She has set all apart to draw all together. With a few draughts from the cup of love she makes good a life full of toil."

Yet there is something in the essay that does not figure in "On Transience," or anywhere else in Freud's writings: a presentiment of eternity. "All is eternally present in [Nature]. . . . She knows nothing of past and future. . . . The present is eternity for her." In this essay, the nature of Nature is strongly personified as a woman, and divine—very nearly as an earthly, maternal stand-in for God. The essay—like the Romanticism of which it was a product—left one wondering whether Nature's power was derived from its own innate sources, or from divine ones.

In a letter written to his friend (and, he hoped, lover) Sidonie von Nádherný, on September 15, 1913, a week after meeting Freud, Rilke praised the same apocryphal essay that had so affected the adolescent Freud some forty years earlier. Rilke wrote that he was sending Nádherný a copy of an essay that had made a wonderful impression on him; it may or may not have been by Goethe. He was amazed by its economy of language, by the way it "silently represents, as if it says everything and takes everything back again, and both come together in one statement."

Reading the essay, one sees what Rilke meant in commenting that the essay "says everything and takes everything back again." The "everything" in question is the essence of Nature—

whether the knowable thing science would make it to be, or the divine unknowable of religious belief. Without making any final pronouncement, "Nature" seems to have it both ways: Nature as an atheistic final authority and as an incarnation of the divine. Perhaps because of this evocative ambiguity, the essay spoke just as strongly to the poet of his vocation as it did to the scientist of his.

2

By the time he was awarded the Goethe Prize, Freud was too ill with cancer to travel to Frankfurt to accept the award in person, so he sent his daughter Anna to deliver his acceptance speech. In his address, he wrote that receiving the prize had made him feel as if he should justify himself before Goethe, and "raise[d] the questions of how *he* would have reacted if his glance . . . had fallen on psycho-analysis." Freud went on to find harbingers of psychoanalytic ideas in passages in Goethe's masterwork *Faust.*

Trying to account for his pious feelings toward Goethe, Freud wrote of the human desire to draw close to great figures of the past, to take them as fathers. He discussed the frustrating mystery surrounding the authorship of Shakespeare's work (Freud said he believed that the plays and sonnets were actually by the Elizabethan nobleman Edward de Vere), and explained the appeal such legendary figures held; people yearn "to acquire affective relations with such men, to add them to the fathers, teachers, exemplars whom we have known or whose influence we have already experienced, in the expectation that their personalities will be just as fine and admirable as those works of art of theirs which we possess." Yet Freud acknowledged that it was not only admiration one felt for one's ancestors: "Our attitude to fathers and teachers is, after all, an ambivalent one since our reverence for them regularly conceals a component of hostile rebellion." In this ambivalent spirit of paying homage to the ancestral fathers to whom he felt he owed allegiance both culturally and personally, Freud, now an elder himself, gratefully accepted the Goethe Prize as a gift from the past, from his literary ancestor.

In keeping with the conventions of his time, Freud's writings are filled with quotations from classical literature. He used them constantly, in his letters as well as his formal work, and as often as they are cited explicitly ("As Plato said . . ."), they appear even more frequently in allusions, off the cuff, giving the reader the impression that the thoughts of the ancients are interchangeable with Freud's own (as, for example, when, allowing for the possibility of telepathy, he cites *Hamlet* and agrees that "there are more things in heaven and earth . . . than are dreamt of in your philosophy"). Such references seem to come to Freud's rescue anytime he starts in a new direction, or tackles an especially difficult problem, or arrives at some point that may be especially obscure (as when, in introducing the idea of a death-drive, he turns first to Plato's myth of the origin of love). Freud often invokes classical quotations as points of reference for readers, to clarify an idea with a familiar signpost, or to put them at ease in strange territory; occasionally, though, the quotations work in the opposite manner, and make what appeared familiar or evident newly subtle, fresh, or even obscure—sometimes in ways hidden to Freud himself. And more than once, Freud summoned the wisdom of the ancients during heated disputes with his closest friends; in his early argument with Jung over the occult, for instance, he compared his skeptical attitude to that of "the poet [who] confronted undeified Nature after the gods of Greece had passed away"—a reference to Friedrich Schiller's "Die Götter Griechenlands."

The works of the great Greek writers, as well as the plays of Shakespeare and the Bible, are frequently pressed into service, as are the works of renowned poets and humorists nearer to Freud's own time. But the work cited more than any other, to which Freud returns again and again for advice and insight, is Goethe's *Faust*. To a person of Freud's time, Goethe was the German Shakespeare, a vernacular literary genius in an age that gloried in the protean capacities of the individual. Like Shakespeare before him, Goethe was regarded not only as the poet most representative of his culture and language, but also as having been a principal force in the creation and transformation of German into a European, literary language.

In contrast to Shakespeare's, however, Goethe's life is extremely well documented—like Freud, he left extensive correspondence, as well as a voluminous autobiography—and his life story was an integral part of his fame. Goethe's rise came early, and nearly overnight, with his publication of *The Sorrows of Young Werther* in 1774. The novel was a sensation throughout Europe, and spawned, along with the new literary genre of the bildungsroman (a coming-of-age novel, typically observing the "storm and stress" of anguished youth), adolescent legions who costumed themselves in Werther's trademark blue and yellow in emulation of the book's unhappy hero. As with Richard Wagner later, Goethe's early popularity was cult-like, an early version of celebrity, and as with modern celebrity, it held up a singular, distorted image of the poet.

Werther's success derived from its portrayal of a youth enraptured and tormented by love. His love, conveyed in a torrent of passionate letters to his beloved, uproots the hero from sense and reason, making him insensible of anything outside his emotional upheaval. When his beloved marries another, Werther kills himself, his suicide note heaping condemnation on a world unmoved by passion. This is *Werther*'s urgent theme, and with it that of all Romanticism: that the world of feeling must triumph over that of reason, though this triumph may be realized only in death.

In 1772, before writing *Werther*, the twenty-two-year-old Goethe had been passionately in love with a woman in his neighborhood, and, anticipating his hero, he sank into an anguished depression when she married her betrothed. Around the same time, he learned of the fate of his friend Karl Wilhelm Jerusalem, who committed suicide out of love for the wife of a government official. From these two experiences—his own anguish and the suicide of another—Goethe fashioned his novel.

In doing so he spared himself the suicide he may well have contemplated, by transferring his feelings to his character, expressing them in the safe middle ground of fiction—and gained adoration and fame in the process.

Freud admired not only Goethe's creativity and his prolific achievements, but also his personality, which, like his own, was that of a bourgeois gentleman—learned, generous, humble, honest, and perhaps above all, forbearing in the face of adversity. Throughout his life, in youth as in maturity, Freud looked to Goethe as a model.

There were striking parallels between the two men's lives. In 1917, returning by train from a vacation in the Tatra Mountains, Freud wrote a short essay analyzing Goethe's first memory, which he had described in his autobiography, *Dichtung und Wahrheit* (*Poetry and Truth*). The memory revolved around a scene of the poet as a child at home, throwing crockery out of a window with a sense of great pleasure. In his essay, Freud interpreted this fragmentary recollection as a "screen memory," and using a method much like the one he had used in analyzing his own screen memory in 1899, showed how Goethe's memory unconsciously expressed, in distorted and nearly unrecognizable form, the child's wish for his new brother's removal (and accordingly the child Goethe's return to prominence in his mother's affection), as well as his satisfaction when his brother really died.

The interpretation was a daring bit of literary sleuthing; it also closely resembled Freud's own infantile relationship and rivalry with his brother Julius, whose importance for his future development Freud had recognized during his self-analysis in the 1890s. Like Goethe's brother, Julius had died in infancy; he had died before Freud's second birthday. And like Goethe, young Freud was able to keep his place as his mother's favorite because of his brother's death. Freud concluded the essay on Goethe's childhood memory by remarking that "if a man has been his mother's undisputed darling he retains throughout life the triumphant feeling" that leads to real success. He had voiced the same sentiment about himself, in his autobiographical study years earlier.

Freud was by no means alone in his feeling of kinship with Goethe, nor was he ignorant of the importance of heroes like Goethe in the development of culture. In *The Psychopathology of Everyday Life,* Freud compared the legendary figures of a culture to infantile memories. "Thus the 'childhood memories' of individuals come in general to acquire the significance of 'screen memories' and in doing so offer a remarkable analogy with the childhood memories that a nation preserves in its store of legends and myths."

3

Faust is the curious culmination of Goethe's literary work. Beginning life as a novella, when Goethe was in his twenties, it became the hobgoblin that would haunt him for the remainder of his long life, that he would take up and leave repeatedly, even as he finished an incredible range of other works, including plays and lyric poetry, fiction and essays. Finally, at the insistence of his friend Friedrich Schiller, Goethe took it up again in the early years of the nineteenth century, and the "first part" was published in 1808. He continued work on the second part until a few months before his death, in March 1832, making sure that it would not be published until he was gone.

The story of Faust was already a popular legend when Goethe took it up, and had been the subject of a previous literary treatment more than a century earlier by Christopher Marlowe. But Goethe transformed the story into something entirely new, a work that combined fiction, poetry, drama, satire, and doggerel in a yearning, bursting sprawl, in the tradition of Rabelais's *Gargantua and Pantagruel*, and Laurence Sterne's *Tristram Shandy*.

Faust is the story of a doctor, a man of science and reason, who, bereft of his faith and goaded by despair, signs over his soul to the devil in exchange for an extraordinary night on the town. The action of Part One (the better-known part of the epic) takes Faust from his own study, to a bawd's tavern, to a witches' lair, to his lover Margarethe's chamber, to a surreal convocation of devils, ghosts, and witches on Walpurgis Night, and finally to a dungeon, where Faust misses, apparently, his last chance for redemption by abandoning the unexpected love of Margarethe and the illegitimate child that she carries for him, and for which she will be killed. And this is only Part One!

Narratively, *Faust* is a mess. The first and second parts, separated in their writing by decades, not only are inconsistent with each other, as are many of Shakespeare's works (especially the histories), but also violently contradict each other on the central matter of Faust's salvation. At the conclusion of Part One, as he rides off again with Mephistopheles, the reader is left with the certainty of Faust's condemnation, a fact reinforced by his own recent cowardice toward Margarethe. Part Two, however, barely mentions the "Faustian bargain" made by its hero for his soul, and the reader is surprised at the end to see the old doctor borne aloft on the wings of angels.

Yet despite its problems of coherence (or perhaps because of them), *Faust*'s heterogeneous, nearly formless form is an apt metaphor for its subject—the creation of a world whose moral center is occupied by the twin forces of creativity and reason. It is a Romantic's rage against the tyranny of the intellect, and an Enlightenment thinker's rage against religion, painting a world in which the forces known to govern the human realm recede before an older one, ruled by magic and alchemy, a world of wishes and dreams. It is also the portrait of an aging writer's battle with his youthful self, the uneasy negotiation of a man with the passionately held positions experience has caused him to relinquish. Finally, it is a faithful portrait of anxious human experience in a world whose very incoherence gives rise to an endless search for explanations, elucidations, and answers—for Truth.

Although Faust's story remained unresolved at the end of Part One, Goethe did not take up his masterpiece again until the last years of his life. Like its predecessor, Part Two is a hodgepodge of different styles, genres, and meters; its method and message are, nevertheless, very different from those of the first. In Part Two, the sinner Faust, having sold his soul out of sheer disdain for his humanity, seems to recover his virtue and have all but forgotten his pact with the devil. As the story careens through battlefields and foreign economies, pagan Olympus and Christian heaven, Faust marches toward redemption. The final lines of the tragedy are cryptic:

Alles Vergängliche
Ist nur ein Gleichnis;
Das Unzulängliche,
Hier wird's Ereignis;
Das Unbeschreibliche,
Hier ist's getan;
Das Ewig-Weibliche
Zieht uns hinan.

All transience
is only a likeness;
the inadequate
becomes event;
the undescribable
is here realized;
the Eternal Womanly
draws us onward.

These lines are ambiguous in German, and almost nonsensical in translation. They are abstract, without an obvious reference to the play's concluding action (Faust's efforts to reclaim land from the ocean, which have resulted in his redemption) or to its main theme (the battle between reason and passion). Puzzled over since Goethe first put them down, they have been interpreted to mean many different things. Some scholars hold them to be an expression of the redemptive power of creativity; Faust, they say, is delivered from his pact with the devil and carried aloft by angels, as a result of his protean efforts to reclaim land from the sea. Others view the lines as Goethe's retraction of his long-held antipathy toward religion—a sort of deathbed conversion.

At the heart of the puzzle is Goethe's strange neologism, *das Ewig-Weibliche,* "the eternal womanly" or "eternal feminine." Nothing in the preceding text or in Goethe's other writings explains clearly the meaning of the phrase. It has been taken to refer to the heroine of *Faust,* Margarethe, whom Faust impregnated and then abandoned at the end of Part One, but who is redeemed with him at the conclusion of Part Two. The Eternal Feminine has been understood also as a maternal divinity, opposed to the orthodox, patriarchal Christianity of Goethe's day. Written in an era when literature was dominated by men, it has been seen as a simple metaphor for desire, for all that makes man strive beyond himself. As it entered the canon of Western literature, Goethe's Eternal Feminine retained its enigmatic character and became shorthand for the obscure nature of creative inspiration and for the human ability to create meanings from language that might exceed easy comprehension.

The Eternal Feminine thus came to stand for two nearly opposing ideas. On the one hand, it represents the creative capacity of the artist, who, through art, transforms his own impulses into a new kind of communication; on the other, it stands for divine inspiration, which forcefully pulls the passive artist along toward whatever art he is destined to create.

In describing the Eternal Feminine, Goethe refers to existence as *"alles Vergängliche."* *Vergänglichkeit,* or transience, is for Goethe as for Freud a name for the human condition; the humanity it evokes is marked by mortality, time-boundedness, and impermanence. The adjective *vergänglich* recalls the word for "mortal," *sterblich,* which means literally "like death" or "having death." In proclaiming, *"Alles Vergängliche ist nur ein Gleichnis"*—all transience is only a likeness—Goethe offers the reader a choice: Either life is an image—a mirage, shimmering and beautiful, but devoid of meaning—or it is a symbol—representing something else besides itself, imbued with meaning by a source beyond itself, by Nature maybe, or by God.

Thus the final poetic lines of *Faust* stage a battle between faith and skepticism, implying that human life may be a symbol for something else—the "undescribable"—that is realized here on earth, led on by the puzzling Eternal Feminine, and thus tantamount to a religion; and at the same time that existence stands for nothing at all, and man's soul is nothing but an empty, deceitful mirage. In these final lines, Goethe seems, paradoxically, to return to *Faust's* original theme (rationality versus romanticism) and to undercut it, by introducing the possibility of divine influence.

When Freud, in preparing his essay for the patriotic anthology *Das Land Goethes,* called it "On Transience," "Vergänglichkeit," the haunting last words of Goethe's masterpiece could not have been far from his mind. They portray a human existence that is fragile and fleeting, its true essence shrouded in mystery or perhaps absent altogether, and whose only certainty lies in the limit imposed on it by death, and yet which is still "led on," driven somehow to perpetuate its living in spite of all. As the guns of Europe rained death and havoc throughout the world that Freud belonged to and cherished, the simultaneously mournful and hopeful sentiments of Goethe's elegiac words must have seemed to him to echo his own as he had expressed them in "On Transience."

Also among the themes embraced by *Faust*'s final lines is another one very close to that of Freud's essay, a theme as close to his heart as it was to that of the poet. Goethe's lines reprise a struggle with which Freud grappled throughout his life, and which he spoke of in his Goethe Prize address—the struggle between artistic and scientific ways of knowing, between intuition and reason.

CHAPTER SIX

Freud entered the University of Vienna in 1873 and, after flirting briefly with studying law, decided on a career in science. Throughout his university years, which he would later remember as the happiest of his life, he excelled in the driven environment of the laboratory, which was then dominated by the renowned scientists Ernst von Brücke and Theodor Meynert, members of the so-called mechanistic school, whose adherents held that life could be approached like a machine, and that nature operated according to changeless, rational laws.

The culmination of hundreds of grueling laboratory hours spent during a fellowship in Trieste in the spring of 1876, Freud's earliest contribution to science was not distinguished by glamour. By dissecting the genitalia of some four hundred eels, he demonstrated the surprising fact of their bisexuality— their possession of reproductive organs that, in maturity and under certain environmental influences, could become either male or female. This early work was a long way from the controversial theories he would announce some twenty years later, which also asserted bisexuality (this time, the psychic bisexuality of humans); far from advancing any theory of his own, Freud's work with eels and their singular reproductive adaptation constituted yet one more confirmation of the speculations of his scientific idol Charles Darwin.

Freud was very proud of this student work, and remained so until the end of his life. He envisioned a career immersed in this kind of science, characterized by painstaking research grounded in precise, objective observation. He could not have known how far from the reassuring certainty of the scientific method his work would take him.

But not long after his university studies were over, financial need forced him to abandon research; as a young man without independent means, he could not sustain an academic career in the Austrian Empire, where young professors were largely expected to support themselves. Faced with this reality, Freud decided to practice medicine.

Freud's subsequent study would take him further and further from strict scientific observation. Since 1884, with his research into the anesthetic properties of cocaine, he had started to employ himself as a subject of experimentation and use his own experience as a source of data. Self-experimentation was not uncommon in the science of Freud's day; early discoveries in the fields of anesthesia and pharmaceuticals, and the therapeutic application of X-rays and other types of radiation were achieved by scientists who took themselves as subjects, often with dire consequences (when Freud was himself a patient seeking relief from cancer, he consulted with the radiologist Guido Holzknecht, whose self-experimentation with X-rays resulted in his grave illness and death). In an age before sophisticated clinical trials, using oneself as a subject of experimentation was not only consistent with the scientist's image as a bold adventurer, but was often the sole way to conduct research.

Freud's experiments with cocaine went on for nearly four years. In those years he prescribed the drug to himself, his friends, even to his fiancée, Martha, for its effects against various kinds of anxiety, and also against physical pain. Later, as he became interested in hypnosis through his studies in Paris with Jean-Martin Charcot, a pioneer in the study of hypnotism, and, subsequently, in his treatment of hysterics, his methods relied ever more on subjective "data," on the intuitive experience of the observer, rather than impartial observation.

Hysterics—patients, mostly women, whose suffering could be traced to no physical illness, and whose symptoms ranged from fatigue to anxiety to blindness and even to catatonia—had long posed a mystery to physicians throughout Europe. The theories offered to explain the sources of their illnesses were nearly as various as the symptoms themselves—ranging from degeneration in the brain or other vital organs to insufficient sexual gratification, which was sometimes treated by the physician's physical stimulation of his patients' sexual organs (the word *hysteria* comes from the Greek for "womb"). Freud's solution was not, in its way, any less strange. "Hysterics," he famously wrote in 1895 in the groundbreaking *Studies on Hysteria,* "suffer mainly from reminiscences."

To relieve the sufferings of such patients, Freud employed a variety of techniques, including hypnosis, suggestion, and the "cathartic" technique, by which, with his hands pressed against their heads, he would try to have patients relive painful events of the past. In 1896, after years of struggling to find a way to work with hysterical patients, Freud arrived at the method of "free association," the heart of psychoanalytic technique. With this new approach, he had his patients say whatever came to mind, no matter how silly or absurd, how improper or awful, it seemed. Over time, through these associations, he believed, he could tease out the repressed, "forgotten" conflicts at the root of a patient's neurosis and free the patient from illness. The patient known as Anna O. came to refer to this curious therapy as the "talking cure," and so it was.

In the 1913 essay "On Beginning the Treatment," Freud explained the technique of free association in psychoanalysis by comparing it to a train ride: "Act as though, for instance, you were a traveler sitting next to the window of a railway carriage and describing to someone inside the carriage the changing views which you see outside." In this image, Freud imagined an internal world, mirroring the outer world of the traveler. Like a commuter who takes an interest in the passing landscape he routinely ignores, in free association the patient is supposed to direct his attention to the trivial, incidental thoughts he takes for granted and regards as unrelated to his goals and problems. These ephemeral thoughts are the key to understanding ourselves, for according to Freud, we overlook them precisely because they are thoughts about feelings, and we regard them as unwelcome, and as having no bearing on the immediate reality with which we are constantly faced. These forces labor unheralded outside our conscious awareness, by a logic that is as inexorable as it is invisible.

The paradox behind "free association" is that it is not free at all. It is, in fact, constrained by the unconscious forces that are the precipitates of a lifetime of conflict. By following the figurative, autobiographical tributaries that make up memory, Freud tried in analysis to discover their source, and thus to understand the constituent elements and motive forces of behavior. Yet the laws so rigorously obeyed by the unconscious do not readily conform to the laws of objective science.

In these later efforts, too, Freud was his own principal subject. By analyzing his dreams, by associating their contents with images of his past, his friends and family, and the sorrows, jealousies, rages, and joys that populated his memory, he developed the techniques and theories on which psychoanalysis would be based. For the scientist in him, this posed a problem.

Freud had been taught that one arrived at and confirmed knowledge by systematic observation, and he embraced his commitment as a researcher to the rigors of the scientific method. In his own work, though, intuition played a critical role: how could talking about emotions be scientific? Freud's

medical colleagues ridiculed his research, which could be neither confirmed nor disproven by independent experiments. He
continued to insist on the scientific validity of his research, often by comparing his psychoanalytic theories to less controversial scientific ideas, such as the laws of gravity, which, like
unconscious processes, could be only inferred, never seen.

Freud could not deny the intuitive nature of his work, but
he refused to allow his theories to rest on intuition alone.
Throughout his working life he sought to reconcile the findings of psychoanalysis with those of biology, hoping to set the
subjective "data" of mental life—dreams, feelings, thoughts—
on a par with the demonstrable and repeatable phenomena of
orthodox science.

Free association had led Freud to believe that for each individual the meanings attributed to events, people, and places
were idiosyncratic, fluid, and interconnected, like the diverse
tributaries of a stream, furrowing their way through the landscape of memory. But what, with certainty, could be known of
their source?

2

In July 1915, Freud completed the last of a series of twelve papers on "metapsychology," the result of his attempt to provide
a theoretical frame for all of his psychoanalytic work. They
were written, he said, to distract him from the cares of the
world raging outside his door, where war continued to deprive

him of his colleagues, family, and livelihood, and they reflect, as he wrote to Lou Andreas-Salomé, "the lack of good cheer in which I wrote them."

Freud had long supposed that his discoveries—unconscious processes, the meaningfulness of dreams, the importance of the instincts and the Oedipus complex—were universal in human experience, and that these phenomena had their roots in mankind's obscure past. In the final paper of the series on metapsychology, "Overview of the Transference Neuroses," he described an incredible natural history of the mind, derived from a conjectured prehistory of mankind. According to Freud's scheme, each of the neuroses encountered in psychoanalysis corresponds to an episode in the saga of primeval events, beginning in the Ice Age, when, as he believed, the human race was ruled by a violent patriach, who forbade his sons to procreate, and castrated them; this hated father, in turn, was eventually overthrown by the rebellious heirs of these sons, who murdered the "primal father" and in his place established civilization among themselves.

In each episode, Freud perceived the roots of one of the mental disorders he described: anxiety, hysteria, and obsession arose during the reign of the father; psychosis and paranoia resulted from the sons' guilty victory over their patriarch; and mourning and melancholia stemmed from the culmination of this history, in the sons' grief for their murdered father. Freud theorized mourning to be the climax of the neuroses, the most recent chapter of an ancient past and the final step toward a civilized present.

He never published the paper in which these ideas were put forward, although he hinted at them in several other publications, most notably in *Totem and Taboo,* issued in 1912 and 1913. The lost twelfth essay, along with six others, was destroyed by Freud, and the collection was never published. The draft of this "phylogenetic fantasy" surfaced in recent times, among Freud's letters to Ferenczi, and was published some seventy years after its author discarded it.

The ideas in this paper, which might seem crazy to the contemporary reader, were strongly influenced by Jean-Baptiste Lamarck, a French naturalist whose work was a precursor to Darwin's. Like Darwin, Lamarck understood natural history to be a process of the adaptation of organisms to their environment. Unlike Darwin, however, Lamarck believed not that it was the happy accident of "natural selection" that determined the course of evolution, but rather that evolution resulted from an organism's intentional alteration of its own body or structure to conform to the demands of the outside world.

The difference between the two theories might be put like this: Assume paleontologists were to find evidence of a human ancestor endowed with six fingers. A Darwinian explanation might be that in the distant past humans had two ancestors, a five-fingered one and a six-fingered one; because the tasks of life (holding a spear, say) were better accomplished with five fingers, our six-fingered relatives all died out, leaving it to those with only five fingers to propagate future generations. Lamarck, instead, might have supposed that, in order to meet those tasks of life more suited to five fingers, our six-fingered ancestors adopted the practice of cutting off the extra member, and by this act of autoamputation produced in their descendants the desired complement of digits.

Science has in large measure borne out Darwin's theories, and it would be difficult today to find a scientist who would advocate Lamarckian views. But for scientists of Freud's generation, educated before the revolution of genetics, the latter were still plausible and passionately argued ideas. No one was more passionate about them than Freud, who saw in them a reflection of his own ideas. For Lamarck as for Freud, memory was life's motivating agent, the force that gave it its shape and sense. For both scientists memory was like blood, a life-giving archive of recollections coursing through the race. Humanity as a whole was the vessel of this mnemonic history, of which individual lives were mere repetitions.

Freud believed the body itself was an organ of history, with memories serving literally as the building blocks of existence—its DNA. In "Instincts and Their Vicissitudes," written in 1915, the same year in which he wrote his phylogenetic fantasy, Freud mentioned approvingly the biological theory that held that individual organisms (including humans) were no more than appendages of an immortal, life-sustaining "germ-plasm" transmitted through propagation from generation to generation. Findings within the field of genetics have in a sense supported this; the codes of DNA, by virtue of their role in determining individual constitution, are in some sense immortal. But they do not carry with them the scars of individual history, the way, for instance, trees do in their rings.

The fateful difference between Lamarck's theories and Darwin's had finally to do with the methods that gave rise to them. Darwin's hypotheses emerged after decades of research in the Galápagos Islands and other far-flung regions, based on close observation of the small differences that distinguished species from one another. They were based, in other words, on observable phenomena. Lamarck, in contrast, depended for the crucial element of his theory on the speculation that history was recorded in the body, though that history had disappeared, never to return. In the end, the triumph of Darwin over Lamarck was the triumph also of observation over intuition—two conflicting ways of knowing, which Freud also struggled to reconcile in his own thinking as he sought to comprehend the human mind's workings and internal battles through the intricate, inevitably subjective methods of psychoanalysis.

3

Although he ultimately rejected it, the hypothesis of Freud's Lamarckian phylogenesis was simple and powerful: All individuals carry with them the whole of human experience. With this, Freud envisioned a transparent universe, one available to total comprehension, in which the past and the future were linked in an endless circle governed by a collective, organic, immortal memory. The impingements of the natural world—climate change, terrestrial catastrophes, epidemics—so critical in the shaping of human development in Darwinian evolution, were relegated to a minor role. The past was written in the body and the blood, and what had been recorded there—the early turmoil of the species—continued to shape humanity in the present, within the individual and in the entire race. Memory was rooted in biology, and as Freud would later notoriously write with respect to female sexuality, "anatomy is destiny."

Freud's phylogenetic hypothesis had another implication, too. For if, at the level of the germ-plasm, the basis for all human experience is within us, then at some level memory outlives us and is immortal in ways that we ourselves are not. Thus memory has, or is, something very near to an afterlife—as near to an afterlife, at least, as Freud would allow.

Freud thought that even the most obscure mysteries might be solved with the help of this collective recollection, which he described to Lou as the "Witch Phylogenesis" (a reference to the scene in *Faust* in which the hero reluctantly seeks help from a witch to learn the secret of eternal youth). In early 1916, in a letter to Ferenczi (who shared in these beliefs), Freud called on Lamarck again. "Don't we now know two conditions for artistic endowment? First, the wealth of phylogenetically transferred material, as with the neurotic; second, a good remnant of the old technique of modifying oneself instead of the outside world (see Lamarck, etc.)." Art, the enigma before which psychoanalysis was normally forced to lay down its arms, became comprehensible to Freud when creativity was chalked up to memory, the deathless agent that enabled one to transform oneself, instead of the world. Rather than allow the present to be driven by the power of buried memories, through the medium of art the past might live again in the light of day, without overshadowing it.

CHAPTER SEVEN

I n the autumn of 1911, Rilke arrived at Duino Castle, near
Trieste, where he had been invited by his friend and patron
Princess Marie von Thurn und Taxis–Hohenlohe. "A body
without much of a soul," the imposing medieval structure
overlooked the Adriatic from a cliff, its stone faces lashed by
the elements. At the end of December, after several weeks in
society with the princess and her entourage, and several more
during which the frustrated poet found his time monopolized
by personal business, Rilke hoped to return to creative work,
the need for which had tormented him since completion of *The
Notebooks of Malte Laurids Brigge.* The opportunity came at
last in January, on the back of a gale-like *bora* blowing over the
Adriatic coast.

Walking outside the castle, while worrying over an important letter, Rilke heard what seemed like a voice speaking
through the wind as though dictating to him. He took down
the words in a notebook, then went inside to finish his letter.

By evening he had completed the first of the elegies that would mark the zenith of his poetry.

Such waves of productivity, and the accompanying barren spells, were the rhythm of Rilke's most creative years. What was new at Duino was the apparently miraculous nature of his inspiration. The princess later recounted the famous legend of the First Elegy's birth, as told to her by the poet:

> *It seemed that from the raging storm a voice had called to him: "Who, if I cried out, would hear me among the angels' hierarchies?"*
>
> *He stood still, listening. "What is that?" he whispered. "What is coming?"*
>
> *Taking out the notebook that he always carried with him, he wrote down these words, together with a few lines that formed by themselves without his intervention. He knew that the god had spoken.*

It seemed to Rilke that "the god," the divine muse of his inspiration, had actually appeared before him, restoring his creativity. The poet's reaction, as he described it in his letters, was ecstatic; it appeared the dry spell was over. But after the creative burst of the ensuing few days (during which he also composed the Second Elegy), Rilke stopped writing again; he was to be mainly silent for most of the next decade. Generous as it was in its abundance, divine inspiration was unspeakably cruel in its absence.

2

Just before this brief creative rebirth, Rilke considered undergoing psychoanalysis to resolve his inhibition. He had often expressed an interest in analysis, which was naturally amplified by his hearing of Lou's experiences in Vienna and her friendship with Freud. Moreover, Rilke's estranged wife, Clara, had been in treatment for several years, and Rilke had been impressed by her reports of its positive effects.

In the last days of 1911, Rilke wrote Lou, after a lapse of nearly four years, to request her advice about whether to seek analysis. He wrote also to Viktor von Gebsattel, the psychoanalyst who had seen Clara Rilke and been Lou's lover, inquiring about the possibility of analysis with him. Gebsattel responded promptly, urging Rilke to begin treatment.

After a letter conveying her initial cautious encouragement, Lou sent Rilke a telegram, followed by a second letter, in which she retracted her approval and emphatically advised the poet against psychoanalysis. Rilke gratefully accepted her judgment. He told her he feared that the palliative effects of analysis would come at the cost of his creativity; and while he had contemplated giving up poetry altogether after the completion of *The Notebooks of Malte Laurids Brigge,* he now preferred the "self-treatment" of writing to the uncertain influences of psychotherapy.

On this point the former lovers were in agreement. They

worried that analysis would, in Rainer's words, correct him with "red ink like a child's exercise in school." In order to "drive out the devils, it would drive out some of the angels too."

Years later, Lou remembered the decision to send the telegram as among the hardest of her life. Since the first days of their liaison, she considered Rilke's afflictions—depression, frequent illness, the perennial chaos of his personal relations, his restless nature, and especially his anguishing inability to write—as symptoms of mental conflict. Even before she knew of Freud or psychoanalysis, she had been convinced of the power exercised by the phantoms of the mind, whose force she had borne ample witness to in her earlier involvements with Nietzsche, Paul Rée, her husband, and Rilke. Now, having embarked on a career in psychoanalysis, she could have little doubt of the origins of Rilke's suffering. Still, she sent her telegram.

In 1912, Lou had not been through analysis herself (as, indeed, she never would). Thus she could offer no guarantee of its benefits from personal experience. On the question of art and its relation to the base impulses of human instinct, her own experience was uncertain. Her early spirituality had led her to suppose that art emerged from an inner inspiration beyond the reach of clinical understanding. Yet as a novelist and poet whose works drew heavily on her life, she must have been aware of the connections between her own experience and the works that so plainly evolved from them. Indeed, once she began working as an analyst she published very little fiction or drama, and even then only allegories of her new analytic ideas.

Writing to Freud in January 1919, Lou expressed a view very different from the psychoanalytic one of the sources of creativity, and of "the pleasurable element in artistic activity: namely, an element which, persisting in the [individual's] narcissism, did not form part of the rest of the [psychological] development. . . . One might almost say: the artist is given something (as a present) before he even wishes for it or noticed the lack of it. He matures through this gift, while other people have to mature by way of their deprivations." By virtue of this "gift," she believed, artists were different from other people, and their artistic impulses stood separate from the rest of their psyche.

Lou's reaction, meant to protect Rainer's creativity, his gift, betrayed her doubt about the source, strength, and nature of the creative impulse, and its fortitude against the corrections of the external world. Looking back, she considered Rainer to have been too far along in his career to be helped, though not to be hurt, by analysis. Rilke's torments belonged to his psyche—but so did his poetry.

3

In 1904, Rilke had been horrified by his friend Ellen Key's biographical interpretations of his work in her preface to an edition of his book *The Stories of God*. Familiar with the poet's helter-skelter, often melodramatic existence, she saw his poetry as an outgrowth of his life's turbulence—and particularly of his relations with Lou, through whom Key knew him. Rilke's letters to Key and others at the time reveal his antagonism toward any effort to regard his poetry as the expression of personal emotion.

For the poet, such interpretations threatened creativity. His poetry, he told Lou, was precisely about transformations of the actual world which, he believed, could supplant the raw materials of emotions, events, and people from which his poems were drawn, making these real things superfluous and irrelevant. Rilke wanted his poetry divorced from real life, that he might fashion actual experience into a new reality—the authorized version of the poet.

The poem "Archaic Torso of Apollo" is typical of Rilke's outlook. Describing an ancient statue, he wrote of the certainty that the "torso still is suffused with brilliance from inside. . . .

Otherwise this stone would seem defaced
beneath the translucent cascade of the shoulders
and would not glisten like a wild beast's fur:

would not, from all the borders of itself,
burst like a star: for here there is no place
that does not see you. You must change your life.

In the ruined ancient statue, and in the caged panther of another famous poem, Rilke perceived an inner experience radically removed from real life, rooted solely in the created self. The change he spoke of had nothing to do with the real world, but involved an internal world that called to him more force-fully than anything beyond it. In the Tenth Elegy, he even speaks of the emotions as though of geography, the real inner landscape that outshines the outer world.

> *... How we squander our hours of pain.*
> *How we gaze beyond them into the bitter duration*
> *to see if they have an end. Though they are really*
> *our winter-enduring foliage, our dark evergreen,*
> *one season in our inner year—not only a season*
> *in time—, but are place and settlement, foundation and soil*
> *and home.*

Psychoanalysis also took the interior world as its subject, striving to enlarge the individual's awareness of those hidden passions that operate as compellingly in their sphere as the more evident motivations to which we normally attribute our actions. For Freud, the turbulent unconscious played as active a role in the formation of one's personal world as anything that might be touched or smelled or seen; through analysis, he hoped to extend human perception to this emotional under-world, joining it with the landscape of everyday feeling, and so enliven each analysand's singular reality.

And in this Rilke sensed danger, because he sought to use the emotions to transform, even to deny or destroy, the visible, consensual world, in order to create poetry. Rilke "treated" the emotional conflicts that raged in him with his art, and pursued this remedy with a consoling single-mindedness, to the exclusion of all others—and to the exclusion too, perhaps, of his well-being.

Rilke's anxiety during the long stretches of barrenness meant that he had lost confidence in his internal direction. Without poetic inspiration, he was thrown back on the disorienting conflict between world and feeling, and became, as he said, "improbable" to himself. Reality conflicted with art because it, too, could not be denied, and because, unlike his poetry, it did not need him, was indifferent to his needs, and so had no point of reference for him. Through the need of his demanding art, Rilke remained the center of the world, and when his art abandoned him, he was set adrift.

In work, Rilke hoped to ward off the dangerous "unreality" of his inner life, from the terrible feeling of emptiness that continually expressed itself as an inability to write. He contemplated psychoanalysis; and yet, even before he heard Lou's answer, he had resolved his problem in the way he knew best, through writing. The elegies had come to his rescue, if only briefly. Had he foreseen this all along? Were his overtures to analysis just a way of scaring himself into working again? Even as Rilke's consideration and eventual refusal of analytic treatment spurred him to renewed inspiration, they seemed to signal his acceptance of the unconscious origins of inspiration, and his fear of the threat posed to creativity by the taming of devils.

4

Rilke's and Lou's apprehension stemmed from their protectiveness of the poet's intuition, that obscure, fragile instrument used to transform the world into words. They feared that psychoanalysis would pit this intuition against the scientific tools of analytical knowledge, and that intuition would lose.

In this antagonism between empirical truth and intuition lay the heart of the poet's unease with psychoanalysis. This conflict had a profound effect on Rilke's conception of his work, and assured its difficulty. For Rilke, writing was an invocation of the muse—even of literal spirits, like the one he believed he had heard at Duino. He depended on the fickle forces of his intuition, and no amount of work could conjure it into being. Intuition preceded work, preceded the lifting of the poet's pencil, and it needed protection from those who sought to penetrate its mystery.

When, in the cold wartime winter of 1916, Rilke refused to see Freud, in a second rejection of psychoanalysis, his need to protect his inspiration was evident in his apologetic letter. "I was often on the point of helping myself up out of the depths by having a talk with you. But finally the decision prevailed to struggle through alone, as far as one still has a miserable shred of solitude left. If I can gradually get some measure of control, then I shall certainly invite myself and come to see you; I know that will be good for me." Only in solitude, by drawing on his own inner resources, could the poet regain his muse. For Rilke

at least, between the enigma of creativity and the psychoanalytic science that would plumb its depths, no lasting bond
could be forged.

5

In the mysteries of creativity, Freud found tantalizing possibilities for insight into human nature. He had recognized precur-
sors of psychoanalytic ideas in the works of great artists, and
had pursued these ancestral connections in his enduring preoccupations with Shakespeare, Goethe, Leonardo, and others.
Freud made the affinity of psychoanalysis with these artists ex-
plicit in his theory of "sublimation," and with it grasped what
he thought was the essential purpose behind the creative
process: Creation was the ingenious triumph of human desires
over the obstacles in reality that opposed, confined, and disappointed them.

He borrowed the term "sublimation" from the language of
chemistry, where it referred to the transformation of a sub-
stance directly from solid to gaseous state. It was the crown
jewel of psychoanalytic theory, and its saving grace. As Freud
himself once winkingly put it: "People say: 'This Freud is an
abominable person; however, he has one rope with the help of
which he can pull himself out of the sewer in which he dwells,
and that is the concept of sublimation.'"

He told colleagues that he came upon the idea while reading

Heinrich Heine, the bilious German Jewish poet and satirist who was, like Goethe, a favorite of his. Freud had read Heine's account of a delinquent boy in the Harz Mountains who went around cutting off the tail of every dog he could get his hands on. When the boy grew up, he became a great surgeon. All the while, Freud remarked, he was doing the same thing; he had merely put his brutality to good use.

Freud thought sublimation to be the best of what is human. It meant turning to good account the worst or most primitive impulses within oneself, harnessing them in the service of culture rather than against it. In Freud's version of human development, the brutality of primitive man gave way to submission to laws; indiscriminate exercise of sexual instincts yielded before the demands of an orderly society. At every step, the advance of civilization entailed a renunciation of individual impulse. Inevitably, such renunciations were not without cost, which was exacted in the form of the neurotic illnesses that were the inchoate protest of individuals against their terrible sacrifice.

The purest form of sublimation was art, which involved the discharge of impulse through symbolic expression rather than action. In a work of art, the artist's own inner struggles were resolved through the act of imagining and creating. *The Sorrows of Young Werther,* for instance, harnessed its author's anguished disappointment in love and transformed it into a narrative with the capacity to move an entire generation.

The process by which sublimation was accomplished was

not at all clear to Freud; his explanations of creativity managed to be both eminently psychoanalytical and a bit mysterious. He was fond of quoting Hamlet's admonition, "There are more things in heaven and earth . . . than are dreamt of in your philosophy," as he did in justifying his open-mindedness toward the possibility of telepathic communication. Admitting the limits of knowledge, Freud wrote, "Before the problem of the creative artist analysis must, alas, lay down its arms."

Nearly from the outset of the analytic enterprise, Freud had conceived of sublimation as a process of channeling sexual instincts to cultural purposes. In 1914 he refined this idea by supposing that the energy of the "object-libido," the instinctual energies normally directed toward other objects, might be withdrawn again into the ego, desexualized, and redirected, often in the service of the "ego ideal" (an internal image of oneself as one wants to be). Sublimation, then, consisted in the transformation of love withdrawn from others into ambition in the world—an impulse that, at the same time it produced effects in the world, enlarged one's sense of self.

6

Freud was fond of remarking that the man who first hurled words, instead of a spear, was the inventor of civilization. In writing or in art, the artist, like Freud's mythical diplomatic savage, found a place of accord between the conflicting impulses within himself and his way to health, as the neurotic did in the symptoms of illness. He did so through the creation of beauty in the world, a human beauty that would rival the achievements of nature.

For Freud, beauty had everything to do with sex. As he understood it, beauty originated as a means of stimulating the visual organ—the eye—to produce sexual excitement in order to facilitate reproduction. As evolution worked its gradual magic, concealing its primal machinery in progressively more complex forms, beauty functioned as a more general, less evidently sexual stimulus. But through all its modifications, its primitive roots remained unaltered.

The experience of beauty, Freud supposed in *Civilization and Its Discontents,* begins in erotic self-observation. The first object to ravish an infant's eyes is his own body, the reservoir of all early appetites and satiation. Later, as he looks beyond himself for satisfaction—to his mother, then others—the infant transfers the pleasure of looking to other things, other people, and eventually, Freud believed, to the objects of civilized beauty.

Freud thought it was these infantile and instinctual roots to which artists, musicians, and poets returned when creating beauty in art. All artists drew from their own store of sexual ("libidinal") energy to produce images or ideas that would satisfy, through this substitute activity, sexual impulses in themselves and in those who witnessed their creations.

There is reason to believe that, for all the explanatory power of his theories, the experience of beauty remained alien to Freud. He said as much in a letter to Wilhelm Fliess (written in 1897, at the beginning of the Italian journey during which he would write of his need for a "punch made from Lethe"):

> *It is my hope to penetrate somewhat more deeply into the art of Italy. I have some notion of your point of view, which seeks not that which is of cultural-historical interest, but absolute beauty in the harmony between ideas and the form in which they are presented, and in the elementary pleasing sensation of space and color.*

Deprived of its historical context—without the aid of museum plaques—Freud had difficulty appreciating the "useless beauty" of paintings, sculpture, or especially, music.

Even in his writings about those artists he most admired, such as Leonardo and Michelangelo, Freud's enjoyment of beauty depended on his ability to analyze it. An exception was his experience of Michelangelo's statue of Moses holding the tablets from Mount Sinai; when Freud was in Rome, he returned repeatedly to San Pietro in Vincoli, the church where the statue sits, and imagined himself one of the Israelites to whom the patriarch offers his scorn and reproach. But even before his favorite sculpture, Freud's appreciation was tempered. At the beginning of his essay about the work, "The Moses of Michelangelo," published anonymously in 1914 (among his favorites of his own writings), Freud wrote:

I have often observed that the subject-matter of works of art has a stronger attraction for me than their formal and technical qualities. . . . Nevertheless, works of art do exercise a powerful effect on me, especially those of literature and sculpture, less often of painting. This has occasioned me, when I have been contemplating such things, to spend a long time before them trying to apprehend them in my own way, i.e. to explain to myself what their effect is due to. Wherever I cannot do this, as for instance with music, I am almost incapable of obtaining any pleasure. Some rationalistic, or perhaps analytic, turn of mind in me rebels against being moved by a thing without knowing why I am thus affected and what it is that affects me.

Freud went on to analyze not the effect of Michelangelo's statue per se, but the image of Moses, the sculptor's subject. That is to say, Freud again approached what he found beautiful using the analytic tools with which he was familiar, while keeping its "powerful effect" at a comfortable distance.

Before experiences of beauty, such as that afforded by art, Freud had declared psychoanalysis powerless. Though he could explain both the creative impulse (by the theory of sublimation) and the effect of art on the viewer (the origin lay in the infant's pleasure in his body), he could not put them together, to account for the transformation of sensual experience into an aesthetic one. And for Freud himself, the beauty of such objects, and the beauty of art, remained coldly inaccessible—except in memory.

In "Screen Memories," the essence of Freud's recollection

had been contained in just those elements (the yellow of the flowers, the taste of the bread) that pertained to the senses, "the elementary pleasing sensation of space and color" to which Freud had declared himself blind to Fliess in 1897.

In October of that year, Freud wrote Fliess of another early memory, of himself as a little boy sobbing before an empty cupboard as his mother rushed into the room to console him. Freud found embedded in this single memory a whole network of his childhood experiences, including fear of his mother's abandonment, rage at the birth of his sister, sexual jealousy of his older brother (whom he believed responsible for his mother's pregnancy), and at bottom, the recollection of the sudden disappearance, when Freud was not yet three, of his nanny ("an ugly, elderly but clever woman, who told me a great deal about God Almighty and hell and who instilled in me a high opinion of my own capacities"), who was jailed for stealing from the Freud family (he thought her incarceration echoed symbolically in his memory of the cupboard). Of this second screen memory and the catalogue of early heartaches that he saw in it, Freud told Fliess: "I cannot describe to you the intellectual beauty of the work." Only in the storehouse of his own recollections—or more precisely, in his unraveling of the endless anguishes they concealed—did Freud recognize the beauty that seemed everywhere else to elude him.

Freud's declared insensitivity to beauty recalls an exchange he had with a friend, the novelist and Nobel laureate Romain Rolland, which he reported in 1930, toward the end of *Civilization and Its Discontents*. Rolland had experienced an unusual emotion that he guessed to be the basis for religious feeling. According to him, this "oceanic feeling" awed its host with a powerful sense of wonder, a flooding vitality that overran reason and evoked a unity with the world. As Freud later described it:

[This sensation] consists in a peculiar feeling, which he [Rolland] himself is never without, which he finds confirmed by many others, and which he may suppose is present in millions of people. It is a feeling which he would like to call a sensation of "eternity," a feeling as of something limitless, unbounded— as it were, "oceanic." This feeling, he adds, is a purely subjective fact, not an article of faith; it brings with it no assurance of personal immortality, but it is the source of the religious energy which is seized upon by the various Churches and religious systems, directed by them into particular channels, and doubtless also exhausted by them. One may, he thinks, rightly call oneself religious on the ground of this oceanic feeling alone, even if one rejects every belief and every illusion.

In letters to Rolland and in *Civilization and Its Discontents*, Freud claimed that he could find no trace of such a feeling in himself, and he declined to analyze too deeply what was beyond his experience. He speculated, however, that the origins of the sensation lay in the infant's original secure union with his mother, and that the experience in later life of Rolland's "oceanic feeling" was really the expression of a longing to be restored to that early unity. The sense of eternity and the urge for union with the world, expressed a longing to merge not, Freud believed, with God, but with the mother from whom one is separated at birth; a yearning not for an ecstatic present, but for a blissful, unremembered past.

In *Civilization and Its Discontents,* contemplating the "oceanic feeling," Freud described this original state of the infant's ego as boundaryless, without distinction between himself and the world around him, and outlined the process by which, under the influence of reality, the infant is gradually separated psychologically from his mother and the outside world.

> *The ego detaches itself from the external world. Or, to put it more correctly, originally the ego includes everything, later it separates off an external world from itself. Our present ego-feeling is, therefore, only a shrunken residue of a much more inclusive—indeed an all embracing—feeling which corresponded to a more intimate bond between the ego and the world about it. If we may assume that there are many people in whose mental life this primary ego-feeling has persisted to a greater or less degree, it would exist in them side by side with the narrower and more sharply demarcated ego-feeling of maturity, like a kind of counterpart to it. In that case, the ideational contents appropriate to it would be precisely those of limitlessness and of a bond with the universe— the same ideas with which my friend elucidated the "oceanic" feeling.*

Freud thought the oceanic experience was an emotional relic of the dawn of life, a memorial feeling that preserved the inner world of the newly born. Alluding perhaps to his own memories of Gisela Fluss, he compared this persistence in the mind of its primitive state to an alligator, the lingering representative on earth of the extinct Saurian race, and further likened the mind to an imaginary Rome, "in which nothing that has once come into existence will have passed away and all the earlier phases of development continue to exist alongside the latest one." In this impossible city of the mind, all the edifices of the past continue to exist alongside those erected later in their place.

At the same time, Freud saw the oceanic feeling as the start of a long process of psychic evolution, which would transform the infant's oceanic feeling into the nicer passions of maturity. At birth, the infant makes no distinction between himself and his mother's body or anything else outside him; only through repeated experiences of frustration of his needs does he gradually discover himself as a separate being. These disappointments are painful, and it is his early tendency to avoid them, either by actions (screaming, movement) or by wishing them away (by hallucinating the nourishing breast, for example), that first prompts the infant to confront the world on his own. (Freud had made poignant illustration of this early worldliness in *Beyond the Pleasure Principle,* in his description of the *"fort-da,"* or "here-gone," game, in which he saw a child—his own grandson—try to control his mother by tossing a ball of yarn and pulling it back to himself, in imitation of her departures and returns.) In this way, the longing to reestablish the old prenatal state of union becomes the first occasion for fantasy, imagination, and creativity—all of which, as the infant matures, come increasingly under the influence of reality.

This imperative to symbolize and translate the external world into his own private language, to re-create loved and needed others within himself, was the first step on the infant's road to communication. The emergent process of symbolic expression was the child's response to the growing recognition of the gulf between himself and others, and the need to preserve what was submerged in this gulf—the sense of unity and of omnipotent well-being with which he had begun life. To bridge this ever more pressing divide between himself and others, he began to take them into himself, recasting them as language or image or object, and so laid down within himself the foundations of culture, religion, art, and science.

Freud uses the concept of oceanic feeling in *Civilization and Its Discontents* to show how humans adapt to reality, by renouncing desires or indulging them, or by the compromise of sublimation—the most desirable yet most difficult solution. In this context, sublimation seems an outgrowth of the "ego-feeling of maturity," an adaptation to reality in accord with the pleasure principle. Or does it?

In a letter to Romain Rolland discussing the oceanic feeling, Freud declared, "I am closed to mysticism [represented by the oceanic feeling] as to music." In asserting his alienation from music, Freud equates the inspiration received from that most abstractly emotional of the arts to the mystical oceanic feeling.

His comments imply that the oceanic feeling—the vestige of the symbiotic experience of earliest infancy—is connected to the creative impulse, and that both lie outside the shaping sphere of normal psychological development, much like the "gift" of creativity that Lou Andreas-Salomé had earlier proposed.

Freud's statements on the nature of the oceanic feeling conflict. In one view, the imperative to survive forces us to renounce our nostalgia for the womb, to pursue our psychological destiny in the "sharply demarcated ego-feeling of maturity." In another, this primal longing persists, safe from the alterations of adaptation, untouched by compromise with the world.

This contradiction extends to the nature of the creative process. For if the oceanic feeling is left behind with infancy, as the subsequent chapter of *Civilization and Its Discontents* suggests, then artistic achievements are the result of the adaptation of desires and wishes to reality. If, however, the oceanic feeling survives unchanged in the mind, then creativity is a short-circuiting of the maturation process, and draws its strength from the artist's fixation in an infantile state of development. In the first case, creativity results from the withdrawal of "object-libido"—love—from the object or lover, and is returned to the ego and used for "higher" purposes. In the second, the source of the inspiration is the lost object preserved in the psyche, in museumlike isolation from the rest of the mind, with no higher purpose than to call out to what is lost.

Freud's rumination on the oceanic feeling suggests two possibilities: creative inspiration emerges either by holding on to the objects of the past inside oneself or by gradually letting them go and replacing them with new ones. The two processes—stubbornly holding on or letting go—parallel those of "normal" mourning (in which, as Freud describes in "On Transience," the libido is gradually withdrawn from the lost object and put to new use) and melancholia, the "revolt in their minds against mourning," in which the loss of the object is denied. ("No! it is impossible that all this loveliness of Nature and Art, of the world of our sensations and of the world outside, will really fade away into nothing," as the poet is paraphrased in the essay.)

Was sublimation more akin to mourning or to melancholia? Was creativity an act of psychical maturity, or a regression to the earliest kind of mental functioning—an act of consummate sanity, or one of psychosis? This ambiguity in Freud's thinking reverberated in his feelings toward art and artists.

As he often did for such experiences, Freud introduced Rolland's "oceanic feeling" with a literary allusion. "If I have understood my friend rightly, he means the same thing by it as the consolation offered by an original and somewhat eccentric dramatist to his hero who is facing a self-inflicted death. 'We cannot fall out of this world.' That is to say, it is a feeling of an indissoluble bond, of being one with the external world as a whole."

The quoted line, from Christian Dietrich Grabbe's play *Hannibal*, was a favorite of Freud's; he had used the phrase in letters to Karl Abraham in August 1914 and Lou Andreas-Salomé in 1915. In the play, Hannibal's remark as he contemplates suicide with his Roman enemy approaching is a consoling thought of immortality—even in death, one cannot "fall out of the world," for death, too, belongs to the world, at least in Grabbe's grand conception. The parallel to the oceanic feeling is obvious, with one difference; Freud connects the feeling not only with the infant's longing for the womb, but also with the equally universal urge to avert mortality and deny the terminus of death.

Consistent with his scientific training, Freud was a committed skeptic; he referred to himself as a "godless Jew," and in later years wrote extensive psychoanalytical refutations of religions (especially the one closest to him). So it is hardly surprising that he could find no trace of the "oceanic feeling"—no sense of eternity or union—in himself. But in his letter to Rolland in which he excused his doubts about the "oceanic feeling," he had concluded that he was as "closed to mysticism as to music." Lumping art and spirituality together, Freud underscored their common roots in a realm beyond reason—an irrational underworld more akin to the primitive urges of our ancestors—more akin, perhaps, to madness.

CHAPTER EIGHT

n *September 1921*, after a long interlude in their correspondence, Rilke sent Lou a recently published book on
Adolf Wölfli, a painter who suffered from mental illness.
Rilke had become fascinated with Wölfli, whose story he
thought offered vital insight into the nature of all artists. Creativity, Rilke suggested to Lou, emanated primarily from two
possible sources: an awareness of an excess of creative forces
welling within one (as he thought was his own case), or in cases
of madness, the interruption of consciousness itself, which
would stimulate an overflow of creativity. Rilke thought this
insight essential for understanding the creative artist, and for
comprehending the symptoms of mental illness, which, like the
eruptions of inspiration, were an effort to restore to harmony
the creative rhythms of nature that the illness had disturbed.

Lou responded immediately, and diplomatically, to Rilke's
letter. She told him she would send the Wölfli book on to
Freud, and she did so not long after. Freud responded with a

letter thanking both Lou and Rilke for the book, without further comment.

Wölfli was a Swiss peasant who spent the last thirty-five years of his life confined to mental hospitals. His artistic inclinations first showed themselves after the onset of his madness, and during the years of his confinement he painted inexhaustibly, as long as he was given materials with which to paint. His efforts eventually yielded several thousand works, depicting events from his own life, from memories of his early childhood to more recent images from his time in the Waldau sanatorium; biblical and mythological imagery; and renderings of such exotic places as Siberia and the Waldorf-Astoria hotel in New York, which he knew only through pictures.

By today's diagnostic criteria, and those of Freud's time, Adolf Wölfli would be classified a schizophrenic, suffering from psychotic symptoms such as hallucinations and paranoia that severed his relationship to reality. Now as then, schizophrenia stands at the limits of understanding. Freud rarely saw schizophrenic patients himself, and he doubted the effectiveness of psychoanalytic methods in such severe cases; he considered them the result of severe narcissistic disturbances, and too primitive to be helped by analysis.

In his own time, the care given to a man like Wölfli was largely custodial; he was locked up and left to his own devices. Comparing himself to this psychotic artist, Rilke reaffirmed his belief that only solitude, and the freedom to give his creativity full rein, could have any therapeutic effect on the miseries that plagued him, and to which he ultimately attributed his writer's block.

In the world of today's psychiatry, Adolf Wölfli would most likely not be spending his life in a mental hospital. He would benefit from the enormous advances in medication that have emerged in the last decades, which have afforded independent and productive lives to many who would otherwise remain prisoners of their illusions and anxieties. But whether he would retain the enormous capacities for artistic creation that accompanied his descent into illness is impossible to say; without the anxieties that his painting controlled and that medication would dispel, Wölfli may well have had no need to paint.

Wölfli's art, as both the book by his psychiatrist, Walter Morgenthaler, and the art itself make clear, was the fruit of Wölfli's ongoing effort to comprehend what was happening within him. The brilliantly colored paintings depict again and again what he called "catastrophes," the bewildering confluences of inner and outer reality through which he felt his illness, in the hallucinations that haunted him. Beautiful as his works often are, they present a world distorted beyond recognition.

2

If Rilke sent Freud (via Lou) the Wölfli book intending it as a message, it was a strong one. Wölfli's work was both an expression and a symptom of his affliction; moreover, it was his psychosis and its influence on his work that generated the considerable interest in his work. Rilke's gesture seemed to confirm his view that analysis might study the relation of the mind of the artist to his work, but only at a distance, like a biographer. Both a self-protective warning and, perhaps, an excuse for his behavior toward Freud, the book drove home the point that for Rilke, life, psychic turmoil, and art were vitally entwined and could not be disentangled without harm to the artist's creativity. In Wölfli, Rilke saw reflected his own struggles as an artist—both in the dislocations of Wölfli's madness and in the effort to preserve his personal humanity through art. Before such a struggle, Rilke appears to imply, it is better to give the artist his own pencils, as Wölfli's minders did, than correct him with the "red ink" of normal sanity.

In his letter acknowledging the gift, Freud referred to the painter as the *"geisteskrank[er] Künstler"*—the spiritually ill artist. The phrase harks back to a time when mental illness was regarded as a degeneration of the soul, or even demonic possession. Freud had rejected the term *geisteskrank* years earlier as a relic, yet in this letter he used it without explanation or question.

A more combative Freud might have politely insisted (as he usually did) on his own theoretical understanding of Wölfli's psychosis as a flight from a world within himself that was too painful to bear. Instead, Freud seemed to defer to Rilke's vision of madness as a sickness of the spirit, of the soul, the road back from which must be achieved on the soul's terms—through art.

Whether Freud's politesse was an act of reconciliation on his part, or a genuine fear for Rilke's creativity, he did not say.

Just after the Wölfli exchange, Rilke sent Lou his introduction to a book of ink drawings by Balthasar Klossowski, the thirteen-year-old son of his lover Baladine (the boy would become famous as the painter Balthus). The images depicted the story of a cat, Mitsou, who wandered into the family household one day, settled in, and then disappeared as abruptly as she had arrived. While he had taken up the project in part as a favor to Baladine, it is very likely also that Rilke saw in the images drawn by this child a connection to Wölfli's paintings. From the innocent as from the insane, Rilke sought guidance and inspiration.

What children and madmen share, as poets have recognized since ancient times, is their exclusion from the fellowship of reason. This shared society, of which Rilke believed himself a member as well, put them irrevocably at odds with psychoanalysis. In his response to the Wölfli book, Freud hinted that he agreed, or at least that he would not insist on a union of psychoanalysis and art. In fact, he had relented years before, shortly after writing "On Transience," when he was first spurned by the poet.

Within months of the Wölfli episode, over a few weeks in early 1922, Rilke finally completed the *Duino Elegies* begun a decade earlier, as well as fifty-five poems in a new cycle, the *Sonnets to Orpheus*. In February, he triumphantly announced their birth to

Lou: "Now I know myself again. For it was like a mutilation of my heart that the elegies weren't there. . . . They are. They are." He copied over the first three elegies and sent them to her. Several weeks later, with the Fifth Elegy (the last to be written) completed, he sent her the rest. The letters that passed between the two during these feverish months would be their last extended exchange.

The Third Elegy takes direct inspiration from psychoanalysis and Rilke's conversations with Lou. Replete with images of guilty fathers, and the yearning blood of mothers, the poem compares passion and creativity to hidden ancient spirits that course through the poet/lover, like repressed sexual impulses seething in the unconscious.

> *It is one thing to sing the beloved. Another, alas, to invoke*
> *the hidden, guilty river-god of the blood.*
> *her young lover, whom she knows from far away—what does*
> *   he know of*
> *the lord of desire who often, up from the depths of his solitude,*
> *even before she could soothe him, as though she didn't exist,*
> *held up his head, ah, dripping with the unknown,*
> *erect, and summoned the night to an endless uproar.*

The poem is a vision of creative self-birth, the "young lover" tracing his formation by "ancient terrors." He speaks of the mother who created and protected him ("Mother, *you* made him small, it was you who started him; / in *your* sight he was new, over his new eyes you arched / the friendly world"),

141

then reverses the womb metaphor to reflect the poet's autonomous creative gestation ("But inside: who could ward off / who could divert, the floods of origin inside him?"), until he

> *loved his interior world, his interior wilderness . . . Into the*
> *powerful source*
> *where his little birth had already been outlived. Loving,*
> *he waded down into more ancient blood, to ravines*
> *where Horror lay, still glutted with his fathers.*

The elegy concludes with an address to a female "you," whose maternal domesticity might serve as a model to stir his creativity, his "primordial time."

Anna Freud returned to another of the poems, the Ninth Elegy, repeatedly as her father recuperated from his painful cancer treatments.

> *. . . why then have to be human—and escaping from fate*
> *keep longing for fate?*

> *. . . because truly being here is so much; because everything here*
> *apparently needs us, this fleeting world, which in some strange*
> *way*
> *keeps calling to us. Us, the most fleeting of all.*
> *Once for each thing. Just once; no more. And we too,*
> *just once. And never again. But to have been*
> *this once, completely, even if only once:*
> *to have been at one with the earth, seems beyond undoing.*

Show him how happy a Thing can be, how innocent and ours
how even lamenting grief purely decides to take form,
serves a Thing, or dies into a Thing—and blissfully
escapes far beyond the violin.—And these Things,
which live by perishing, know you are praising them; transient,
they look to us for deliverance: us, the most transient of all.
They want us to change them, utterly, in our invisible heart.
within—oh endlessly—within us! Whoever we may be at last.

The Tenth Duino Elegy depicts a young man, recently dead, as he passes through the decaying ruins of a city, on his way to a mountainous afterworld, in the company of a ghostly "Lament" as guide. The "Things" Rilke speaks of in the Ninth Elegy as being memorialized by their naming (in poetry) are set up in the Tenth among the constellations, the interior ones that console and remember them, even in the death that is their most intimate companion.

These "Things" are the constituents of an interior universe that the poet invokes throughout the cycle, and his entire oeuvre, an inner space created by art, independent of reality and mortality. Together, the Elegies imagine an eternally mournful world where, paradoxically, nothing dies, because they are immortalized—constellations in a heaven of art. They are a powerful statement of Rilke's insistent vision of the artist's absolute reliance on his own inner experience, independent of reality or reason.

3

After Rilke's Christmastime visit to the Freud household in 1915, Freud remarked laconically in a letter to Lou that his son Ernst had encountered "his hero Rilke" during a recent visit to Vienna. "But not at our house. Rilke was not to be persuaded to visit us a second time, though his first visit before his call-up had been so very cordial." Several months later, on hearing of Rilke's discharge from military service and his unheralded departure from Vienna, Freud wrote Lou that Rilke had "made it quite clear to us that 'no lasting [bond] can be forged' with him."

Freud borrowed the phrase "no lasting bond . . ."—"*kein ewiger Bund zu flechten*"—from Friedrich Schiller's "Das Lied von der Glocke" ("The Song of the Bell"). This long poem is a panoramic yet elliptical glance over a town's fortunes as a community builds, burns, harvests, revolts, dies, and is born anew. Through it all looms the figure of a bell, Concordia (Harmony), which the townspeople have cast to speak to heaven for them through its song. The casting of the bell signifies the sweeping enterprise of life; and in the bell's pealing, the hearer is reminded of life's essential, contradictory significance:

Only to grave and lasting things,
Be consecrate her metal chime;
And hourly with his rapid wings,
Shall she be touched by flying time.
A tongue to destiny shall she lend;

Heartless herself to joy or grief,
Still with her swing let her attend
Upon the changeful game of life.
And as the sounds which forth she casts,
In mighty tones, on the ear decay;
So let her teach that nothing lasts—
That all things earthly die away.

The bell, whose creation is the culminating result of human labor and life, heralds in its clangor the essential transience of life, the inevitability of death as the end of the "changeful game" and the realization of the poem's epigraph: *"Vivos voco. / Mortuos plango. / Fulgura frango"*—"I celebrate the living / I mourn the dead / I break the lightning." More than a statement of a bell's very functions, the Latin triplet (a customary inscription on bells) is an illuminating metaphor for the functions of mourning. An instrument in the rituals of joy and grief, the bell is also proof against the dangers the indifferent natural world brings, as for instance the stroke of lightning that threatens the town with annihilation.

The passage from which Freud borrowed appears midway through the poem, as a father surveys his family and estate with pride. "Boasting, he gazes round, / 'Firm as the very ground, / Spite of misfortune's cross, / Stands the wealth of my house.'" But the man knows he deceives himself with these transient satisfactions: "With the powers of destiny / No lasting bond may forged be; / And misfortune strideth swift." The bell in Schiller's poem stands against these powers of destiny as humanity's desperate rejoinder to what the Greeks (and Freud after them) called *ananke*—necessity—the single force that our collective ingenuity cannot dominate. It is the emblem of all human striving against the inevitable decline and extinction we face, individually and as a race; it is, to borrow another of Freud's favorite lines, from Goethe, "the best of what you know [, which] cannot, after all, be told to boys"—to the innocent—for it is a knowledge won only by the experience of loss and the intimation that death alone conveys. The bell stands, in a word, for poetry, by which an artist shoulders both the burden of creation and the even heavier knowledge of the transient fate of that creation—and yet takes it up anyway.

4

Freud considered Schiller both an exemplary man and an exemplary artist, and one whose creative nature was altogether different from that of the painter Wölfli, so admired by Rilke. Indeed, in a discussion of artistic psychopathology among the Vienna Psycho-analytical Society in 1909, he praised Schiller as "a particularly fine example of a normal man."

Some years after Schiller's death, Goethe wrote an epilogue to "Das Lied von der Glocke" as a tribute to his beloved friend. The poem laments Schiller's departure, but it envisions his spirit advancing into eternity, while in the life that remains "Behind him, a shadowy illusion / Lay what holds us all in bondage— the things that are common." This triumphal image of the poet shedding his mortal frame to assume his immortal place in history amounts nearly to a refutation of the very poem it celebrates. Goethe looks to eternity for consolation, through the immortality of the poet's writing. It is not life itself, or its limited duration, that gives life purpose; rather, one obtains immortality through one's efforts, bypassing mortality altogether, which is a "shadowy illusion"—or, as he will say at the end of *Faust,* only "a likeness."

In his self-analysis, Freud recalled Goethe's "shadowy illusion," which he took to be a depreciation of mortal existence, and found in it an expression of his own wish to die on his terms, and to leave his children with an image of himself strong and unsullied by the infirmity of age. But viewed alongside the poem that inspired it, what Goethe meant as a tribute to his friend verges on betrayal, by misinterpreting Schiller's theme (creativity as a way to come to terms with human mortality) and turning it into its opposite (creativity as a way *around* mortality) and thus rendering it toothless. This was a peculiar act of friendship, and one that resounded in the exchange between Freud and Rilke a century afterward.

In response to Freud's wounded report that "no lasting bond can be forged" with Rilke, Lou was apologetic on the poet's behalf. "No, do not misinterpret Rainer's attitude. It was not due to any estrangement on his part, but only to his shattered state of mind. I know quite well what he really feels about you."

So, one suspects, did Freud. In his allusion to Schiller, he seems cagily (and perhaps a little competitively) to use his literary knowledge to put his finger on the matter: No lasting bond could be forged with the "powers of destiny"—that is, with Rilke, whose poetic force Freud admired and perhaps feared.

Later in this letter, Freud compares Rilke's creative process, indirectly, to his own. "[Rilke], whom I should like to congratulate on having regained his poetic freedom, made it quite clear to us in Vienna that 'no lasting [bond] can be forged with him.' Cordial as he was on his first visit, we have not been able to persuade him to pay us a second."

Freud continues: "I should have felt sure of myself throughout my life if I could have been sure of my productive capacity at all times and in all moods. Unfortunately, this has never been the case. There have always been days in between when nothing would come and when I have been in danger of losing all ability to work and to struggle, owing to certain minor fluctuations in mood and physical health. A most unsuitable condition for one who is no artist and doesn't aim at being one." Creative blockage, he implies, is the proper domain of the artist. Taking himself to task, Freud discovers in himself the work inhibitions of an artist, but not the inspiration that fuels it.

Lou disputed Freud's self-appraisal. "Although you definitely disclaim the possession of an 'artistic' temperament, to which such interruptions might more readily be supposed to occur, it nevertheless seems doubtful whether an achievement such as yours would have been at all possible if that factor had been so entirely lacking. And in any case your keen enjoyment of works of plastic art [a reference to Freud's avid collection of antiquities] shows that you do in fact possess it to a large degree."

Freud did not respond to Lou's remarks, and would repeatedly deny any artistic element in his work and his personality. But taken in this context, the "powers of destiny" represented by Rilke are not merely abstract: they are the forces of artistic inspiration and poetic freedom. Freud congratulates Rilke's recovery of his "poetic freedom," even as deplores his own "unsuitable" inhibitions; Rilke's rejection of their bond thus seemed to confirm Freud's view of himself as lost to art.

A further aspect of Freud's choice of Schiller to convey his disappointment is indicated in a letter he wrote to Lou in February 1918. Commenting on the recent revolution in Russia, Freud remarked, "What the human beast needs above all is restraint. In short, one grows reactionary, just as incidentally did the rebel Schiller in the face of the French Revolution." Though he is referring to politics here, his use of the poet to evoke his own tendency to reaction is striking. Despite his passion for classical and Romantic poetry and art, Freud remained uncomprehending, even uninterested, in the modernist art that emerged during the second half of his life (though he wrote several times to Lou of his children's passion for Rilke's poetry, Freud never praised the work himself). Freud, the romantic childhood poet, had become in maturity a reactionary, in poetry as in politics—and Rilke was his French Revolution.

Knowing of his admiration for Goethe and Schiller, one can speculate that in quoting "Das Lied von der Glocke," Freud mourned the demise of his relationship with a kindred spirit, especially one whose preoccupations with love and death, inwardness, and phenomena beyond normal perception were much like his own. Freud embraced the view of the inextricably entwined nature of existence and art that was expressed in Schiller's poem but apparently rejected in Goethe's epilogue, as it was also in the young poet's dismissal of the value of mortal life in "On Transience," and perhaps even in Rilke's fear of psychoanalysis. For Freud, as for Schiller, poetry and life were bound together inescapably in time. It is eternity, and the "eternal" nature of art, that is illusory. What gives both meaning, sense, and vitality is the certainty of death.

CHAPTER NINE

Not far into *The Notebooks of Malte Laurids Brigge*, Rilke sounds his novel's theme in a harrowing account of the death of the hero's grandfather.

Christoph Detlev's death had been in residence at Ulsgaard for many, many days now, and spoke to everyone and made demands. Demanded to be carried, demanded the Blue Room, demanded the Little Salon ... demanded the dogs, demanded that people laugh, talk, play and keep still, and all of these at once. Demanded to see friends, women, and people who had already died, demanded to die itself: demanded. Demanded and screamed ...

This was not the death of some ordinary mortal suffering from dropsy, it was the evil, princely death that the Chamberlain had carried and nursed with himself his whole life long. ...

*How Chamberlain Brigge would have looked at anyone
who asked of him that he die a different death. He died his
death hard.*

Malte, Rilke's hero and fictional alter ego, admired his grandfather's violent death, which consumed all those around him,
because it was his own death, or the one he was meant to have.
A death of one's own, both Malte and his creator believed, was
the key to personal freedom.

Years later, in the Fourth Elegy, Rilke returned to the idea of
a death of one's own:

*Murderers are easy
to understand. But this: that one can contain
death, the whole of death, even before
life has begun, can hold it to one's heart
gently, and not refuse to go on living,
is inexpressible.*

2

Rilke was born barely a year after the death of his parents' first
child, a girl, who had died not long after birth. As a child, René
was dressed by his mother, Sophie, in girls' clothes; she let his
hair grow long and called him her "little girl." Over her husband's protests, she treated René this way until he began

school. He soon came to understand the advantages of his role. Once, fearing punishment for some transgression, Rilke donned a dress and assured his mother that "René is a no-good. I sent him away. Girls are after all so much nicer."

Fragments like this from Rilke's childhood suggest that he was a "replacement child." Prevalent in an era of high infant mortality (though not absent in our own time), the replacement child is conceived by its bereaved parents in the wake of the death of a previous child. Such a child becomes the parents' consolation for the loss, but also the reincarnation of the predecessor, along with the hopes and dreams the first child represented.

One widely remarked replacement child is Vincent van Gogh. Like many parents in nineteenth-century Europe, Vincent's lost their first child, a son, a year before Vincent's birth; the dead child's name was also Vincent, and the boys had the same birthday besides. Little Vincent, who lived with his family in the rectory of his minister father's parish, passed his brother's grave, marked with his own name and birth date, every day as he walked to school. As he grew up, van Gogh was the constant subject of unfavorable comparisons with his deceased older brother. In his subsequent, feverish existence, van Gogh repeatedly looked for relief in purpose and human connection. From his early career as a minister to his violent suicide, he sought this redemption through atonement and self-punishment. He was incapable of lasting emotional relationships, except with his younger brother, Theo. Even his paintings—in their depictions of brittle landscapes and impassive attitudes; in the radiant violence of the natural world and the often toylike quality of his human subjects—have come to be viewed as the expression of the genius of alienation, a spirit at odds with the world and with the human community for whom the work of art exists.

Though a child may enter the world under such circumstances and thrive, he may become like van Gogh the unfortunate witness to his parents' disowned grief for the dead sibling. A replacement child shares his identity with a ghost, so that within the space of one growing being there are two.

Every child is greeted at birth by the dreams and hopes and expectations of his parents. His "creators," they plan itineraries for the course his life will take, which echo their own wishes and hopes, or even those of their ancestors. These plans are nothing less than his forebears' bid for immortality, and it is the child's fate to contend with them and, ultimately, in some measure acquiesce to or reject them; most likely, he will do both. In a sense, then, we are all replacement children, and our personalities heirs to the anxieties and desires of those who raise us.

But for the true replacement child, the burden borne is connected with the resurrection of the dead. To conceive a child after another has died is an effort to put biology itself in the service of the denial of mourning. For the unlucky heirs of such a legacy, the result may be damnation. At the very least, they will struggle mightily, in order to separate themselves enough from their parents, and from their doppelgänger, to find themselves.

The replacement child is the example par excellence of an individual haunted by the ghosts of grief. But not everyone is overwhelmed by them. The accounts of Rilke's childhood, and of his life as a girl, which read like fairy tales, spring from his own pen. And while there is no reason to doubt their truth, one can also see in them the poet's own reflection. As he wrote about his youth, which he did throughout his life—his relationship with his mother, his years in military school—he *rewrote* it, making these early torments ever more familiar features of his experience, his life, his story. In his writing, Rilke re-created what was unbearable in his early life and wove from these re-creations the themes that preoccupied him throughout his career—especially his insistence on the preeminence of the interior world he created in his poetry over external experience. But his gifts as a poet came at a terrible price: for when faced with the demands of that real world, Rilke was overwhelmed.

Death was a constant preoccupation in Rilke's work from very early on, less as a fear of personal extinction than as an aesthetic companion, which he seemed nearly to admire, as expressing some limit or ultimate ambition for his art. In November 1915, as Freud was writing "On Transience," Rilke described death in a letter to a friend as "banished and excommunicated" from life, cast out of human thought by fear. He characterized death as only a horizon for life, existing in a dialectical, continuous relation with it. (It is perhaps telling that in the same letter Rilke recommended to his correspondent a biological treatise on life and death by Wilhelm Fliess, the confidant of Freud's conquistador days whose work he eventually rejected as unscientific and far removed from his own.)

Rilke's grief over the early deaths of friends—the artist Paula Modersohn-Becker and the scholar Norbert von Hellingrath—was accompanied at every step by his idealization of the experience of death as a noble, vital challenge or journey, of paramount importance to artistic achievement. The poet's romanticized visions were paralleled by his apparent belief that one could make poetry of one's own death, as one could of one's life, that death was a work one might carefully shape.

But his own end was nothing like what Rilke would have wanted for himself. In 1926, after a lifetime of fragile health, Rilke's constitution finally failed him. In the summer of that year he collapsed; in September, he was diagnosed with leukemia, for which there was no treatment at the time.

Rilke's symptoms had appeared with increasing regularity during the last several years of his life. But despite innumerable medical tests, and obvious physical manifestations, such as the excruciating mouth abscesses and ulcers that regularly sent him to the dentist's chair, his physicians repeatedly diagnosed his symptoms as primarily psychological, just as they, and even Lou, had done for years.

As the symptoms of his physical pain grew, Rilke increasingly feared a mental breakdown. He wrote Lou of his conviction that his difficulties were the product of excessive *Onanie*, or masturbation, a "spilling out" of the force needed for life.

In this explanation, he was drawing on the widespread pre-psychoanalytic idea of neurasthenia. According to early theories of neurasthenia, sexual energy was part of the life force; while this force was properly expended in "normal" sexual relations, masturbation wasted it, and drained one of life. Rilke had been unwilling to submit himself to psychoanalysis for his psychological complaints—his depressions and inability to work—but he was prepared at the end of his life to blame his very physical illness on pseudo-psychological causes. Though Rilke's masturbation diagnosis was horribly wrong in a literal sense, there was a truth in it. Denying the reality of his illness by blaming it on masturbation, he sidestepped reality, and refused to confront and mourn his approaching death. His "onanism" had nothing to do with his illness or his death, but it was symptomatic of the way he lived his life.

Consigned to a sanatorium, Rilke saw no one in his last days save doctors and nurses, his friend and confidante Nanny Wunderly, and Evgenya (Genia) Chernosvitov, the young woman who was his caretaker and secretary. Neither family (including Clara, whom he had not seen in nearly a decade) nor friends besides Wunderly were permitted to visit. In the few letters he wrote, he spoke not of the beauty and transformation of death, but of pain, fear, and his desire to live. His terror before death, the mystery that had long fascinated him and suffused his work, overcame him in the end.

In his last letter to Lou—the only person he asked to be informed of his situation—Rilke wrote bluntly of the "I don't know how many hells" his suffering caused him. When she referred to the letter in her memoirs, Rilke's family accused her of fabricating it; she withdrew the reference from subsequent editions, even though she had Rilke's letter in his unmistakable handwriting before her.

At the end, as the seriousness of his illness became clear, Rilke's friends withheld from him news of his condition. Lou, advised of his doctor's recommendation to keep the truth from the poet, wrote him in words that encouraged his optimism. Till the end, Rilke apparently believed that he would be cured. When the death that he had so extravagantly admired in his writing finally took him, it came by surprise.

3

Rose, pure contradiction, joy
to be nobody's sleep under so many eyelids.

Rilke composed these lines in October 1925, a little more than a year before his death, and immediately recognized in them his own epitaph. In keeping with his wishes, they were carved into his tombstone in Switzerland, near the twelfth-century château de Muzot, the home of his last years.

At the time he composed these lines, Rilke was unaware of his leukemia, and he had no idea that his own death might be imminent. Yet not long before the onset of his final illness, Rilke pricked his finger while picking a rose from his garden (to give to a woman in whom he was then interested). The wound became infected, and the infection soon spread through his arm. Though it had nothing to do with his leukemia, the small wound may have initiated the chain of events that led to Rilke's death.

The legend of Rilke's death was spun from these facts. The poet died, it was said, from the prick of a rose plucked in love; he was killed, that is, by the power of his own feelings. The image of a poet who dies by the force of love is a compelling one, and one that parallels Rilke's own romanticism, especially in the overheated works of his youth. But it bears no resemblance to the reality of his death.

In writing his own epitaph, making death beautiful with beautiful words, Rilke once again appeared to welcome the prospect of his death. Posterity continued this tradition, ennobling Rilke's death with burnished legends, loving portraits, and visits to his grave (strewn with the roses that killed him). His actual death, with its hells of pain and the final terror, was obscured.

4

Five months after Rilke's death, in May 1927, Freud thanked Lou for her recent birthday wishes with the gloom he customarily showed on such occasions: "With me crabbed age has arrived—a state of total disillusionment, whose sterility is comparable to a lunar landscape, an inner ice age. But perhaps the central fire is not yet extinguished, the sterility only affects peripheral layers, and later perhaps, if there is time, another eruption may come." He continued, "I regret that I know so much less about you than I used to do. What new gifts does life bring with it? Mostly negative things, losses, also of people, of whom one has possessed a part."

Lou responded with a long letter. The "eruptions" of youth were "splendid benefactions, and our grateful memory of them can never really die away. But apart from this . . . it seems to me as if old age requites the losses, the lavas, with deeper movements, which are not so easy to record from without."

She then considered the changed landscape of old age, after the loss of erotic feeling. It seemed to her a new childhood, a "vast expanse" full of renewed identification with the surrounding world, in which one might "forget one's personality." Her thoughts turned to Rilke, whose death had evoked in her something "new and unexpected," which she also linked to her old age. In youth, she wrote, she would have experienced death simply as deprivation and loss. But after Rainer's death, "the immediate consequence was unceasing preoccupation with him"; he had become suddenly clear to her in "the totality of his essential character," in a way that seemed to surpass earthly existence. This "preoccupation" came first with grief, because she could not share with him his new, paradoxical vitality. But grief was soon replaced by awe.

She likened her novel experience of Rilke's memory to her sense of nature. She had always felt a need to live in the country, she wrote, because she thought that nature was "telling me, in her trees and meadows and clouds, what she [nature] herself had experienced. . . . And now it is almost as if Rainer were standing under my trees, as they experience autumn or summer or winter or spring." Like the communicative natural world, Rilke in death had become "immutably real and mature . . . and yet symbolizing completely our inner emotions, just as our impressions of external nature are always regarded by us as symbolic of something within us."

Lou found this experience hard to explain, and she regretted that "talking about it does not bring clarity." But she had wanted to tell Freud of it since Rainer's death. "In the old days—how long ago it is—I tried now and then to express the same thing when I wrote or talked to you. For somehow or other it always has been and still is connected with what I learnt to see, recognize and experience through you. That fact is always present to me. . . . It forms the enormous bond which I have always had and always shall have with you."

In death, Rilke, the lover of Lou's youth, had become for the aging woman a luminous memento of a larger existence. Beyond grief, he had risen inside Lou in his "totality," living on in her and through her in an inner communion, like an incarnation of nature itself. Intriguingly, this new "relationship" with Rilke seemed to Lou akin to the connection she had always felt with Freud, since their first meetings in the years before the Great War. The "enormous bond" she felt with Freud, through all that he had inspired in her, had brought her close to nature, to life itself, and even to Rilke's memory.

Responding to Freud's mournful opinion that old age brought

no "new gifts," but only loss, Lou countered that consolation lay not in the "eruptions" of physical life, but in memory, where the beloved dead could become still more of themselves than in life, "immutably," forever.

The strange feelings she struggled to convey to Freud, and of which she felt him to be somehow the source, were impetus for the book Lou published the following year about her relationship with Rilke, the first in a series of memoirs that occupied her at the end of her life. She had written such a book before, after her experience with Nietzsche. And several years later, its grateful nature evident even in its title (*Mein Dank an Freud*— My Thanks to Freud), she would do the same for another friend.

5

Rilke had admired Freud, but ultimately he fled from psychoanalysis for fear that it would exorcise the creative spirit from him. Freud admired Rilke, but his regard, too, had its limits. In an obituary of Lou Andreas-Salomé written in 1937, referring to him for the last time, Freud characterized Rilke as "the great poet, who was a little helpless in facing life." Freud knew enough of Rilke's life, and death, to understand that, no less than the young poet he had written of in "On Transience," Rilke's refusal to mourn—to acknowledge the inevitability of loss—had sent him running from human relationship into poetry, which proved an exquisite but inadequate shelter from the winds of change.

Freud was not wholly a stranger to the poet's attitude. In 1898, shortly after an Easter vacation he took with his brother to Venice and the Adriatic, Freud had a puzzling dream. In the dream, which was accompanied by a sense of dread, he was in a castle, observing enemy warships approaching the harbor. The governor in control of the castle instructed Freud to care for his family, then dropped dead; though he was witness to it, the dreaming Freud felt "no special emotion" about the death. He then saw the ominous ships come into the harbor. Among them was an odd boat, "cut off in a way." It was, he realized, the "breakfast ship."

Freud recognized the vessel as a sinking ship and as a symbol of death. It resembled a black Etruscan ladies' toilet set he had recently seen, which reminded him of breakfast china, which in turn he associated to the word "toilette," which he thought referred to the customary black mourning dress of the time. The "breakfast ship" also recalled the brothers' recent Adriatic crossing, in which they had taken their breakfast on deck. Freud concluded that the governor's death represented his own, and that this was the source of the dread in the dream, though it is exactly where he had no feelings. The feelings he should have had—horror and grief at his own death—had been detached from the contents of the dream, because, as feelings, they were unbearable. And so Freud's apprehension of his own death took the form of an obscure, insensible dream, sparing him the painful contemplation of his death.

The castle in the dream was Duino, beneath whose walls Freud had passed during the crossing on his recent journey. It was the same place where, fourteen years later, Rilke would hear in the wind the first words of his Elegies, in which he imagined death as an interior transformation.

In the end, before his own death, perhaps even in his poetry, Rilke deceived himself and made others complicit in his deception. While in dreams he, too, might have longed to deny death, Freud would not allow himself to fall into the same error.

CHAPTER TEN

For all his superstitions about dying suddenly by fate's decree, Freud's death was neither sudden nor magically motivated. It was heavy and slow and agonizing, and at its root was Freud's greatest sensual pleasure.

In February 1923, when he was sixty-six, Freud noticed painful sores in his mouth. These were soon diagnosed as cancer, with which he would struggle for more than fifteen years. Normally a great retailer of his physical ailments in correspondence, Freud at first told no one of his discovery. But in late April, he reported to his friend Ernest Jones: "I detected two months ago a leucoplastic growth on my jaw and palate [on the] right side, which I had removed on the 20th." His initial self-diagnosis of epithelioma was confirmed by his physician, and arrangements were made for surgery to remove the cancerous tissue.

Freud's cancer had originated in his jaw, and it soon spread to the mucous membrane of his mouth. The first surgery removed the entire lower right section of his jaw, but failed to stop the cancer. During the next fifteen years, it surfaced repeatedly, requiring ever more drastic measures to combat it. By the time of his death, Freud had endured half a dozen radiation treatments—a therapy then only beginning to come into use—and more than half of his jaw had been removed, replaced by prostheses that would be enlarged and painfully adjusted many times, as successive operations cut deeper into his mouth. Eventually his speech was impaired, and the eloquent conversation for which he was famous rendered barely intelligible.

Freud had noticed signs of his illness some five years before the first operation. In a letter to Sándor Ferenczi in November 1917, he remarked on "a painful swelling of my gums (carcinoma? etc.)," which, he said, disappeared upon his availing himself of a patient's recent gift of a box of cigars. Though he understood the implications of his discovery, Freud ignored them.

It could not have escaped his sense of irony that the source of his cancer was the main joy of his life. For his entire career, Freud smoked about twenty cigars daily; he attributed the greatest part of his creative industry to smoking, and despite several rather halfhearted efforts to stop, he was never able to give it up. The psychoanalyst in him understood well enough the unconscious sexual roots of his addiction; yet he understood even better the limits to the freedom from desire that psychoanalysis could offer. His unwillingness to heed the first signs of cancer was an intimate, personal decision, for in that moment Freud chose to retain the dangerous habit he prized rather than prolong his life by renouncing it.

Freud's cancer was not the only health problem attributed to his smoking. In an 1893 letter to Wilhelm Fliess, in which he discussed the cardiac episodes that threatened his health in the years before *The Interpretation of Dreams,* Freud wrote: "I am not obeying your order not to smoke; do you really consider it a remarkable boon to live a great many years in misery?" He would repeat this sentiment, in much the same words, more than thirty years later, when the cancer had already done much of its deadly work.

However foolhardy it appears in hindsight, Freud's decision to continue smoking must have seemed to him a logical outgrowth of his conviction that life's value is not a pure calculation, but an essential personal choice. For Freud, it was the ability to enjoy life through love and work that determined its value. He was resolved to live to the fullest of his capacities—no matter the cost.

2

Soon after the initial surgery, and with his doctor's approval, Freud and his daughter Anna took a long-anticipated trip to Italy, spending two weeks at the Hotel Du Lac in Lavarone before going on to Rome. It was the last time he would venture far from home, until exile forced him from it altogether, and the pleasures of the journey were frustrated by the terrible pain that was now his constant companion. In the letters he wrote during the trip, Freud described his sense of it as a valediction, a coda to his experience of a place that had held his fascination since childhood.

In consultation with his friends, Freud's physician decided to keep from him until his return the news that more radical surgery lay in store. Upon learning this, Freud, adamant about knowing the truth of his condition, dismissed the doctor. He did not discover the complicity of his friends until fifteen years later.

This willful deception was a terrible betrayal to Freud. As a physician himself, he had regarded illness as belonging in the province of reason, and he approached his own case with the utmost objectivity—in part, no doubt, to control his cancer the best he could, by understanding it scientifically; but also as a way, perhaps, of defending against the larger fears that his grave illness presented, of which there could be no comprehension. As much as possible, Freud intended to remain the master of his life.

When told that he would require a tenth operation (there would eventually be thirty-one), Freud at first refused. His colleagues took him to the bedside of his former patient Guido Holzknecht, the radiologist who had investigated the therapeutic use of X-rays by experimenting on himself, and whose limbs had been mutilated by cancer as a result. Freud told Holzknecht that he would refuse further surgery. Holzknecht replied, "What should I say? I will be operated on tomorrow for the twenty-fifth time," and recommended that Freud have the surgery. Moved, Freud told the younger man, "You are to be admired for the way you bear your fate," and Holzknecht

answered, "You know that I have only you to thank for that."
After their meeting, Freud remarked, "We have visited a real
hero. Of course, I will be operated on tomorrow."

Freud had admired such stoicism before. During his only
trip to America, in 1909, he had spent an afternoon at Harvard
in the company of William James, the famed psychologist and
brother of the novelist Henry James. While he and Freud were
walking together, James suffered an attack of angina, and he
asked Freud to walk ahead while he recovered. James's action
made a great impression on Freud, who hoped "that I might be
as fearless as he was in the face of approaching death."

3

In April 1927, Freud wrote his friend and benefactress Princess
Marie Bonaparte of Greece and Denmark: "I am still walking
in the gardens, it is a pity that one has to become old to discover
these pleasures. Do you know the poem by our [Ludwig]
Uhland? I don't remember all of it, but it seems to me to best
capture the mood of spring:

> *The world grows lovelier each day*
> *We do not know what still may come*
> *The flowering will not end,*
> *The farthest, deepest valley is abloom*
> *Now, dear heart, forget your torment*
> *Now everything, everything, must change."*

In the same way he had sought years before to comfort the young poet in "On Transience" with his celebration of nature's impermanence, Freud, beset by the agonies of his disease, comforted himself with Uhland's poem. Even more than in nature's renewable blooming, Freud found comfort in the very naturalness of death, its clockwork inevitability.

Yet his sufferings took their toll, and at times he could not conceal his despair. In 1935, he wrote to Lou: "What an amount of good naturedness and humor is needed to endure the gruesomeness of growing old. The garden outside and the flowers in the room are beautiful, but the spring is, as we say in Vienna, a *Fopperei* [mockery]." And in 1937, in response to an inquiry from Princess Marie, he expressed a very different version of the thoughts he had voiced in "On Transience":

Immortality evidently means to a writer the being loved by many unknown people. Now I know I shall not mourn your death, for you will long survive me. And I hope you will soon console yourself over my death and let me go on living in your friendly recollections—the only kind of limited immortality I recognize.

The moment one inquires about the sense or value of life one is sick, since objectively neither of them has any existence. In doing so one is only admitting a surplus of unsatisfied libido, and then something else must happen, a sort of fermenting, for it to lead to grief and depression. These explanations of mine are certainly not on a grand scale, perhaps because I am too pessimistic. There is going through my head an adver-

*tisement which I think is the boldest and most successful
American one I know of. "Why live, when you can be buried
for ten dollars?"*

Freud's openness to the ultimate mystery of the world, its
"sense or value" so evident in his earlier writings, and especially
in "On Transience," had been tempered by the desperate skepticism of the dying. The "scarcity value in time" that he had proposed in 1915 as a yardstick for life's value had lost its objective
existence, and the loss made him "sick." Whether this sickness
was a revulsion against grief and depression is not clear, but its
source is unmistakable: he no longer had "oceans of time."

Freud managed, however, to end his letter to the Princess
with a joke. *Why live, when you can be buried for ten dollars?*
By mocking the notion of value, the joke made his point again:
Life could not be reduced to a base exchange.

4

On April 9, 1938, Freud noted in his diary the completion of
his and Anna's translation of *Topsy,* a short book in French by
Princess Marie Bonaparte. It was the first translation Freud had
undertaken since his efforts as a young man to render into
German the learned works of John Stuart Mill and the French
pioneers of hypnosis Jean-Martin Charcot and Hippolyte Bern-
heim. Worlds away from such heady scholarship, *Topsy* is the
story of Princess Marie's chow chow.

Dogs were Freud's constant companions in his last decade. The many accounts of his patients testify to the persistent presence of his dogs, usually chows, who lay at his feet while he worked. According to some patients, the fate of their analysis depended on the attitude the dog took toward them. "I think that if the chow hadn't liked me, I would have left," the American poet H.D. (Hilda Doolittle), who saw Freud for analysis, wrote in her memoir. Many of Freud's letters, principally those to women, report on the health and activities of his dogs, which seem to have interested him far more than the events of his own life.

Freud's first chow, Jo-Fie, was a gift from Princess Marie; his ready attachment to the dog was cut short by her death after being struck by a train. She was replaced by Yu, called Lun. They were often joined at the Freud house by Wolf, Anna's Alsatian.

The class and the era in which Freud lived in Western Europe were dog-crazy. Among the urban bourgeois, the domesticated canine was the perfect complement to the examined life, the civilized man's simple savage. Freud himself marveled at dogs' most unhuman capacity for loyalty and unencumbered affection, the freedom from ambivalence that made them the enviable picture of good mental health.

In 1936, Princess Marie's chow was found to have developed a lymphosarcoma on the right side of her oral cavity. Because her owner had patronized Marie Curie's research, Topsy was the first dog to receive experimental radiation treatments then being developed. After lengthy treatment, Topsy's cancer was cured. Freud and Anna undertook their lighthearted translation as he convalesced from the latest round of his own painful therapy, which included some of the same treatments Topsy had received. The parallels between Freud's illness and the dog's are striking, and point to the secret effort at work in this translation. In *Topsy*, Freud could look from a distance at his own failing life, free of the angst involved in contemplating his own mortality.

Lyrical and melancholy, *Topsy* is both a celebration of life and an elegy for the departed. In its short chapters, the Princess imagines Topsy's world, free of human concerns about the past and future, grounded firmly in the delights of life, and burdened neither by painful memory nor by fear of death. Anchored in the present, Topsy draws no conclusions from experience other than the pleasure or the pain of the present; she has no intimation of a time when "now" will cease to be.

5

In an introduction to a new edition of *Topsy* published some forty years after her father's death, Anna Freud remembered his affection for his dogs. "He admired them for their gracefulness, loyalty and fidelity. He often said, 'Dogs love their friends and bite their enemies. Men always mix love with hate.'" Freud loved dogs for this apparent lack of the ambivalence that so complicated human feelings.

In the course of her analysis with him, Princess Marie once reported to Freud a passing thought that ran against everything else she felt toward the ailing Topsy: "I wish that she were dead." Freud responded, "Topsy has been unfaithful to you [by becoming ill], and you are angry at her, and yet since you also love Topsy, your passion is ambivalent . . . whence your desires of death against her." He continued: "In the [*Symposium*], Alcibiades, enamored of Socrates, expresses a parallel attitude. He is motivated by moral rationalizations, but in reality it is the essential ambivalence of all violent love that [he] expresses."

Alcibiades is the last guest to arrive at the banquet that concludes Plato's *Symposium*. He arrives drunk and belligerent, and is offered a seat beside his former lover, Socrates, and their host, Agathon. Flying into a rage, Alcibiades denounces Socrates' inconstancy, his pursuit of superficial beauty, which has led him to abandon Alcibiades in favor of Agathon. Socrates begs his colleagues to defend him against the violence that he fears from his old lover.

In the course of the *Symposium*, each of the assembled guests delivers his opinion about love, and Alcibiades, too, is asked to speak. He warns the assembly of Socrates' prowess in deceit, and protests that it is really he, Alcibiades, who needs defending against his beloved. He praises Socrates extravagantly for his virtues as an orator, warrior, drinker, and thinker. At the same time, he declares that he would like to kill Socrates, because of Socrates' rejection of his overtures, and out of jealousy for the affection the philosopher now showers on Agathon.

Freud had already alluded to the "case" of Alcibiades in 1909, in explaining the importance of ambivalence in the formation of neurotic illnesses. It seemed to him that every love was mixed with hate, and that as a consequence of the lover's exhausting struggle against his ambivalence—against his hatred toward his lover—neurotic symptoms arose to express the banished feeling, while preventing the dangerous emotion from reaching its true object.

In reminding the Princess about Alcibiades' ambivalent outburst, Freud was making a point: It is the fate of love to be bound up with its opposite, and thus even the most unblemished affection—even puppy love—is a battleground of mixed emotions. This ensures that the course of a love affair is never without pain, least of all in the face of death. Bound up as it is inescapably with hate, with all the guilt feelings that hate entails, the fate of love in the event of the loss of the loved one is doubly painful.

6

In a short passage toward the end of *Topsy* titled "Topsy and Shakespeare," the Princess makes plain her envy of her chow's happy ignorance. Topsy's naiveté leaves her free of anxiety, while men struggle to find a place for themselves amid the infinity of time and space. Our lot is the more tragic, for like shipwrecked sailors, in our desperation we grasp at any passing flotsam as though it were a life raft; and we cling to nothing so fiercely as fame. "In this way, our only too real carnal mortality seeks compensation in the imaginary immortality of a name."

The passage goes on to mock the value of the names and works of Shakespeare, Caesar, and Homer; of what use are their words, their works, when "their brains are dissolved" in death? "And even if, in his work, a little of the creator's soul survives at the end of the millennia accorded to earth, this remainder of life would also be extinguished."

In the Freuds' rendering of this bleak vision, in the place of "carnal mortality" (*"mortalité charnelle"*) one reads "bodily transience" (*"leibliche Vergänglichkeit"*). For a translation that is in most respects faithful to the original, this is a striking liberty that transforms a phrase of brutal, almost contemptuous precision into one of surpassing tenderness. It was 1938, and it would be the last time Freud used the word "transience" in print.

One wonders what Freud made of the passage. The advantage of Topsy's canine ignorance, like that of the dead of the underworld, lies in oblivion of death. The tragic vision of humanity invoked by Princess Marie—her certainty that consciousness makes a mockery of life by letting us know death and fear it—is the same one that haunted the young poet a quarter-century before, against Freud's passionate remonstrance and despite his diagnosis of the poet's ennui as a sign of his refusal of mourning. Now, after so much time, after the deaths of both the young poet and the taciturn companion, and as he faced a death each day more imminent, the old man found himself again the ventriloquist's puppet, mouthing the sentiments of his absent adversary.

The passage concludes: "That is why Topsy, whose happiness is confined to the narrow limits of each day, is wiser than I, she who simply inhales the scented June air, whilst I strive laboriously to trace vain signs on this paper."

7

In 1956, seventeen years after Freud's death, Princess Marie Bonaparte published a paper titled, in translation, "Two Thinkers Before the Abyss." In it she translated "On Transience" into French and added to it a recollection from her analysis with Freud. "Everything will perish—he said to me one day—human thought like man. His thought will survive the man twenty or thirty years, but it will die in its turn." The Princess disagreed, citing the example of Homer, who is still read three thousand years later. Freud was unmoved: "Why should a thing that emanates from man endure on that account, when everything in the universe must perish?" Bonaparte told him that she thought what he said was good, but sad, to which he replied, "Why sad? It is the way of life. It is precisely its eternal flow that renders it beautiful."

Only once, the Princess said, had she seen Freud gripped by the "foretaste of mourning" he had spoken of in "On Transience." In a 1936 letter thanking her for a little book "that raised the problem of life and death," Freud wrote: "And if, in your youth of fifty-four years, you cannot avoid thinking whether death will come, which is obvious to me at eighty years and some, [why must I] demand that I attain the age of my father and my brother or pass them, to the age of my mother [who died at ninety-five]? Now I find myself caught in the conflict between the desire for rest, the advent of new sufferings that go with the prolongation of life or the anticipated suffering of separation from all that one has." The little book was *Topsy,* whose translation rekindled for Freud the feelings he had expressed much earlier in his little essay on transience; only this time, the "foretaste of mourning" presaged Freud's own death.

CHAPTER ELEVEN

As *cancer ate* at Freud's body, fascism was consuming the place and culture in which he had passed his life. By 1937, the waiting room at Berggasse 19 was virtually deserted, like the streets outside; the façade was draped with a large swastika; the psychoanalytic press he had founded was shut down; and the books he had written, along with those by Heine, Buber, and Schnitzler, were burned in summer bonfires, even their warmth of use to no one.

Through it all, Freud exhibited the self-control that had distinguished him his whole life; his agitation betrayed him only in small breaches of habit. Martin Freud recalls his father listening to the family radio only once in his life, when Hitler announced the Anschluss joining Austria to Germany. Shortly before the family's departure from Vienna, Anna was taken by the Gestapo for interrogation; prepared for the worst, the family doctor handed her a cyanide capsule. For a full day they heard nothing from her; when she finally returned, Freud was seen to wipe away tears, the first the family had ever seen from him.

The Freuds abandoned Vienna in the late spring of 1938, going first to Paris, in a harrowing overnight train ride, and then to London, where Freud spent his final year. The exodus was made possible by an international effort involving Albert Einstein, Thomas Mann, Romain Rolland, and the U.S. ambassadors to England and France. At a time when Jews in Austria were no longer allowed to leave their homes, Freud's achievements, his fame and influence, were all that protected his family; even so, he could not ensure their safety.

In London, Freud eventually made a new home at 20 Maresfield Gardens. Several months after his arrival, he responded to a British newspaper that had solicited his opinion on the rise of anti-Semitism. In his letter, Freud movingly demonstrated again, this time in perfect English, the steely dignity with which he lived:

To the Editor of Time and Tide:

I came to Vienna as a child of 4 years from a small town in Moravia. After 78 years of assiduous work I had to leave my home, saw the Scientific Society I had founded, dissolved, our institutions destroyed, our Printing Press ('Verlag') taken over by the invaders, the books I had published confiscated or reduced to pulp, my children expelled from their professions. Don't you think you ought to reserve the columns of your special number for the utterances of non-Jewish people, less personally involved than myself?

*In this connection my mind gets hold of an old French
saying:*

*Le bruit est pour le fat
La plainte est pour le sot;
L'honnête homme trompé
S'en va et ne dit mot.*

'A fuss becomes the Fop
A Fool's complaints are heard;
A Gentleman betrayed
Departs without a word.'

*I feel deeply affected by the passage in your letter ac-
knowledging 'a certain growth of anti-semitism even in this
country'. Ought this present persecution [of Jews in Ger-
many] not rather give rise to a wave of sympathy in this
country?*
Respectfully yours
Sigm. Freud.

2

Freud's office in London was a replica of the one in Vienna; to
the extent that his friends and family were able to undermine
the Nazis' wholesale looting of his possessions, everything

appeared as it had at Berggasse 19. Only the garden (which reminded Freud of his childhood in Freiburg) and the window that gave onto it betrayed the shattering change that had taken place.

Freud had been uncertain whether he would be able to take with him the collection of antiquities that populated his Vienna office. He arrived in London with only a figure of Athena; the small sculpture had stood at the front of his desk since it was given to him by Princess Marie Bonaparte. Freud had summed up his feelings for the figure to the poet H.D., to whom he showed his collection at the start of her analysis, with a slyly phallic remark: "She is perfect," he said, "only she has lost her spear." In the end, in exchange for a ransom paid to the Nazis by Princess Marie, the other figures joined their collector.

In Vienna, Freud had assembled his ancient ensemble painstakingly, and the collection had grown with his fortunes. He acquired the first of the objects in 1896, during his first trip to Florence, two months after his father's death. The two plaster reproductions, one of them a copy of a Michelangelo statue, were, he wrote to Wilhelm Fliess, "a source of extraordinary invigoration" for him. Later, as his interest in collecting became more focused, Freud concentrated his attentions on earlier periods of antiquity. He insisted on the authenticity of these acquisitions, and took considerable care to establish their provenance, often carrying them himself to the antiquities department of Vienna's renowned Kunsthistorisches Museum for authentication.

Among his collection were a small statue of the two-faced

Roman god Janus; an Egyptian sphinx amulet (he also had a Greek sphinx statue); a Roman intaglio, or signet, ring, similar to ones he gave to the members of the "Committee" who guarded his interests within the psychoanalytic movement; several mummy statues and burial wrappings with inscriptions from the Egyptian Book of the Dead; a sculpture of a Chinese scholar, which enjoyed a proud place on his desk beside Athena; and assorted vases, reliefs, and figurines. Though he acquired many of them himself, friends and admirers often demonstrated their affection with additions to his collection, which eventually grew to several hundred pieces, encompassing Roman, Greek, Egyptian, Chinese, and Indian antiquity.

Freud took great pride in these artifacts. In 1931 he remarked to his friend the writer Stefan Zweig, "I have sacrificed a great deal for my collection of Greek, Egyptian and Roman antiquities, and actually have read more archaeology than psychology." Each time he acquired a new piece, he would set it before himself on his desk for several days, and even bring it to the dinner table in the family rooms adjoining his offices and admire it as he ate.

In 1916, Lou had seen in Freud's "keen enjoyment of works of plastic art" evidence of the artist in him. But in his own writings, Freud spoke often of archaeology as a metaphor for his own methods. To his patient known as the Wolf Man, Freud said that "the psychoanalyst, like the archaeologist in his excavation, must uncover layer after layer of the patient's psyche, before coming to the deepest, most valuable treasures." In *Civilization and Its Discontents*, Freud imagined the mind as a supernatural Rome, whose present structures coexisted simultaneously with all the cities that had preceded it on that spot. In his discussion of the case of his patient "Dora," Freud compared memories to "the priceless though mutilated relics of antiquity. I have restored what is missing, taking the best models known to me from other analyses; but like a conscientious archaeologist, I have not omitted to mention in each case where the authentic parts end and my constructions begin." The power of memories, like that of artifacts, lay in their entombment. When excavated, an artifact, preserved for centuries, began instantly to decay in its renewed contact with sun and air, at the same time that its beauty, hitherto unavailable to sight, emerged from its concealment. Likewise, Freud believed, the power of memories dissipated when those memories were brought to light, into consciousness. Only in the unconscious did memories have the power that moved one to neurosis, or to dreams. It was the work of the analyst, like that of the archaeologist, to disinter the buried memories, restore to them the voice their repression had denied them, and so deprive them of their dangerous influence.

For all its metaphorical resonance, Freud's love of archaeology was also a boyish romance. His life spanned the first great romantic age of archaeology, the age of Heinrich Schliemann (discoverer, in 1873, of Troy, and later of what he believed was Agamemnon's tomb in Mycenae) and Howard Carter (who unsealed Tutankhamen's tomb in 1922)—men who, unlike Freud's more empirically minded idols, such as Darwin or his old teacher Ernst von Brücke, were not painstaking, objective scientists, but adventurers in search of a history to which they hoped to attach their names. These men were, as Freud once wrote of himself, "conquistadors," heroes of intellect and spirit alike.

Freud prized his artifacts for their connection to the ancient civilizations whose authors he admired and had drawn from in his own work. His interest in archaeology was inspired by the Romantic fascination for antiquity, which found typical expression in poems such as Keats's "Ode on a Grecian Urn" and Shelley's "Ozymandias," in which artifacts embody a connection between the lost past and the present, its oblivious epigone.

Freud was not ignorant of the fragility and ephemeral nature of these cherished survivors of the past, and even as he contemplated his own perilous exile, he worried about their fate. Despite the larger crisis looming over Europe—including the uncertain future of his four sisters in Austria, who would eventually perish in Nazi concentration camps—Freud's statues mattered to him.

These remnants of forgotten gods and ways of life, extinct species, and dead languages appealed to him precisely for their evanescence. They were brittle, fragile survivors of lost time, the last palpable links to a past that had vanished forever, and a reminder, perhaps, of the date stamp of his own life.

In his old age Freud often told guests that he felt closer to his ancestors in antiquity than to his contemporaries. He once pointed to the works of Plato and Homer, Shakespeare and Goethe, and, flanked by idols of Athena, Eros, Osiris, and Amon-Re, proclaimed to a visitor, "Here are my respondents," as though all his efforts had been directed to them. At times, he seemed to identify with his artifacts.

In 1928, years after the "Committee" had disbanded, Freud sent his colleague Ernst Simmel an intaglio ring from his collection as a token of appreciation. In a letter accompanying the ring, Freud explained his symbolic invitation to join a group that, after all, no longer existed. "Forms may pass away, but their meaning can survive them and seek to express themselves [*sic*] in other forms. So please don't be disturbed by the fact that this ring signifies a regression to something that no longer exists, and wear it for many years as a memory of your cordially devoted [Freud]." The old man hoped that the ancient ring, once an emblem of solidarity and friendship, might stand in the future "for many years as a memory" of himself—a part of himself that, he implied, might live on after his own form passed away.

3

During his last months in London, Freud lived as he had always done. He saw patients and worked every day in his office.

But he had fewer patients, and he wrote and read less and less. Everything—every conversation, every page—had its companion in pain.

Among the books he read was *The Emperor, the Sages and Death*, a fictional dialogue on mortality between a rabbi and an emperor at a thirteenth-century court. He thanked its author, Rachel Berdach, for the book, in a letter: "Judging by the priority you grant to death, one has to conclude you are very young." (In fact, Berdach was sixty when she wrote the novel, but had conceived it when in her twenties.)

In his discussion of Freud's illness, his physician, Max Schur, remarked that "the final phase began when reading became difficult." In July 1939, Freud closed his practice. He did not have the energy to write, and he slept fitfully most of the time. Reading was his final refuge, and that, too, he soon gave up, overwhelmed by the pain of the rapidly advancing cancer.

The last book Freud read was an early novel by Honoré de Balzac, *Le peau de chagrin* (*The Wild Ass's Skin*). The novel's hero, like Faust, makes a pact with the devil for his soul, in return for which he receives the enchanted skin of a wild ass. The skin fulfills all its wearer's wishes, but with the realization of each new wish it shrinks closer about him. The hero attempts to master his desires, but he cannot, and he is finally consumed by the ass's skin. When he finished the novel, Freud remarked to his doctor, "This was the proper book for me to read; it deals with shrinking and starvation." Closing his last book, Freud decided it was time to die.

4

Throughout his protracted illness, Freud refused strong pain-killers like morphine, which would have dulled not only his pain but also his intellect. He knew firsthand the dangers of morphine. During his early experiments with cocaine, he had prescribed the drug to Ernst Fleischl von Marxow, a friend and colleague who had become addicted to morphine after a laboratory accident; Freud hoped the cocaine would combat the morphine addiction, but Fleischl von Marxow became addicted to cocaine as well, and this may have hastened his death. Having been witness to the pleasures and the ravages of narcotics, Freud refused drugs. Though his pain was often unbearable, the tortures his illness subjected him to did not deter him: he resolved to remain himself to the end, and to keep his reason.

In Max Schur, Freud had selected a physician who not only appreciated psychoanalytic ideas but also would honor what then, as now, was a controversial wish of Freud's: to determine the time and circumstance of his own death. When they first met in 1928, Freud directed Schur to be truthful with him; he insisted that "when the time comes, you won't let me suffer unnecessarily." On September 21, 1939, sleepless, unable to read, hardly able to move, he summoned his physician for the last time. "Dear Schur, doubtless you remember our first conversation. Now all is torture and it has no more sense." (*"Das ist jetzt nur noch Quälerai und hat keinen Sinn mehr."*) Later that afternoon, Schur administered his patient a small dose of morphine, and he lapsed into a coma. Freud died on September 23, at three in the morning.

In his book detailing Freud's difficult end, Schur reports that he gave him a two-milligram dose of morphine, and then another twelve hours later; Freud would thus have died after a legal dose, the amount routinely administered to alleviate pain.

Yet in early drafts of his manuscript, and in notes made immediately after Freud's death, Schur reported a dose not of two milligrams but of three—a lethal amount for a patient in Freud's weakened condition. The notes reveal further that in those last twelve hours, he administered the dose not twice but three times—again, more than was safe. Before publishing his memoir, Schur consulted a lawyer; he subsequently misreported the dosage and frequency, because, while he had followed his patient's express wishes, he was liable to prosecution for euthanasia.

Freud's death was, in today's idiom, an assisted suicide, committed in an era that did not discuss such a matter openly. To the end, Freud was adamant that his own life have sense—*Sinn*—and that he remain his life's agent. Of the many people whose deaths he witnessed or mourned, those he admired—among them William James, Guido Holzknecht, Karl Abraham, and the mysterious poet of Lavarone—all remained themselves to the last.

5

Das hat keinen Sinn mehr.
It has no more sense.

Sinn is one of those dense words, especially common in German, that stand ambiguously for many things at once. It can mean soul, mind, sense, interpretation, taste, essence, and meaning—an ambitious failure of a word that tries to capture the unnamable essence of human being. As well as any word, *Sinn* embodies the "scarcity value in time" that Freud spoke of in "On Transience"—the balance struck between the blind desire to live and the painfulness of existence. At the end of that essay, Freud wrote of our human ability to replace what we have lost, as long as we are young and healthy. A fighter to the end, Freud understood when the fight no longer had meaning.

His work had been devoted to *Sinn,* to finding sense in the human feelings and subjective experience that make the world one's own, causing us to love, and to desire to understand ourselves by understanding the world beyond us. Like his childhood hero Don Quixote, Freud harbored an impossible ambition: where Quixote sought to live in the world of his dreams, Freud hoped to restore dream life to its rightful home in reality.

Dying at the age of eighty-three, Freud was fortunate to have lived a long life on his own terms. Not all had been so lucky. He outlived many of his younger friends and much of his family. Sándor Ferenczi—after Jung, Freud's closest colleague—had suffered from pernicious anemia, which Freud believed to be at the root of his erratic behavior and unorthodox methods in his final years, during which he alienated himself from Freud and other analysts. Others had suffered terrible delusions in their final moments. Freud's student Viktor Tausk, another of Lou Andreas-Salomé's lovers, gruesomely took his life by simultaneously shooting and hanging himself. Freud's daughter Sophie had been felled by disease, just at the moment when it seemed to her father that her life was at its fullest. Worst of all to Freud was the fate of his father, who had lost control of his bowels and other bodily functions in his last hours, and thus died stripped of his dignity.

After his mother's death in 1930, Freud wrote to Sándor Ferenczi of its impact. "It has had a strange effect on me, this great event. No pain, no mourning, which can probably be explained by the secondary circumstances, the advanced age, the sympathy with her helplessness at the end. At the same time a feeling of liberation, of being set free, that I also think I understand. I was not permitted to die as long as she was alive, and now I may. Somehow, in deeper layers, the values of life will have been markedly changed."

Freud regarded his own death with serenity. He had the satisfaction of seeing psychoanalysis founded and flourishing, and his family spreading into its next generation. Until the end, his mind remained active, as he worked on new ideas, including the beginnings of a far-reaching revision of his theory. He died as he wished, vital and unbowed, as Goethe had said of Schiller, by the "shadowy illusion [that] holds us all in bondage."

6

In *Beyond the Pleasure Principle,* begun in 1919 with cancer growing undetected inside him, Freud proposed his most controversial idea, the "death-drive." Observing that death is a universal phenomenon, he reasoned there must be a force acting to achieve "death," to return life to its original, inanimate form. The death Freud envisioned, however, was not the dreaded death of nothingness, but inertia—a state of consummate rest, in which an organism attains an exhausted equilibrium. For Freud, this static death came first, preceding life itself; in death, by returning to this original, inorganic state, life was brought full circle, to its beginning. Through the death-drive, death had its *Sinn,* and the "scarcity value" of mortal existence was redeemed in the eternal decay and rebirth of life's entropic circuit.

Still, Freud never relinquished the attitude he expressed in "On Transience." In May 1923, as he was undergoing radiation for his cancer, Anna Freud, then twenty-seven, wrote Lou Andreas-Salomé of a memory from a painful time. In September 1917, her family had vacationed in the Tatra Mountains. Walking with her father, in awe of the beauty of their surroundings (which Freud called a "cold paradise"), Anna wished aloud that they could remain there forever, and that everything would stay just as it was in that instant. Much as he had done with the young poet and the taciturn friend of "On Transience," her father replied, "That would hinder pleasure. One enjoys the moment, *because* it is transient." The idea struck Anna as strange and senseless.

In her letter to Lou, Anna considered the problem further. Since childhood she had longed for stillness and eternity. She had believed existence to be like a carriage or automobile ride; life simply passes one by, and one does not begin to live until one gets out and walks around. She reminded Lou of a past conversation about the landscape of Friesland, Germany's rugged coast on the North Sea. Anna had thought it beautiful, because of the nothingness she sensed beyond it, as though something grand, secret, and true began where the land ended. Her childish thoughts seemed nonsense to her now, and when she read *Beyond the Pleasure Principle* it struck her that the eternity and peace she had longed for was death itself.

Amid these melancholy reflections, Anna yearned for the consolation of Rilke's Ninth Duino Elegy, where the poet wondered:

> . . . *how even lamenting grief purely decides to take form,*
> *serves as a Thing, or dies into a Thing,—and blissfully*
> *escapes far beyond the violin.—And these Things,*
> *which live by perishing, know you are praising them; transient,*
> *they look to us for deliverance: us, the most transient of all.*

As she explained in her next letter, Anna believed that the Ninth Elegy's images of a "'rope maker in Rome and the potter by the Nile' stand for the ineffable and inexpressible, because only the simplest and most visible things are able to contain them." She was reminded of Lou's belief that a child's understanding of God comes closest to the truth.

In response, taking up Anna's childhood vision of eternity, Lou suggested an image of her own. With his desire to make what he loves permanent, she wrote, man feels himself like a runner, racing to catch up with what is being lost. But he doesn't sit passively in a wagon, he drives the horse or motor forward, and so it was with human transience (*Vergänglichkeit*). Mortal existence could not be lifted above the withering and rotting of death; it was inseparable from the cycle of conception, creation, birth, death, and resurrection. Even death was only a boundary of experience, which might be joined to life in an image of fullness and eternity such as Anna had pictured, and like the Nirvana of Indian religion, it encompassed both positive and negative within it.

Discussing Freud's attitude toward his (presumed) imminent death alongside Rilke's idealized images of mortality, Anna's and Lou's letters poignantly capture their love and admiration for the two men, even as they struggle with their ideas. Lou's metaphor of the runner reveals a point of view similar to but distinct from both Freud's and Rilke's. Living, she seems to suggest, is too often mistakenly dedicated to outrunning death, a futile attempt to stop the clock. Rather, life should be lived in the moment, without regard to permanence and immortality. Lou thought death was only a boundary to a more encompassing experience, and not simply an end to life.

Freud considered Lou an "'understander' *par excellence*," and throughout their relationship he contrasted her impulse to synthesize and unify with his own tendencies. "The unity of this world seems to me so self-evident as not to need emphasis. What interests me is the separation and breaking up into its component parts of what would otherwise revert to an inchoate mass."

For Lou, *Sinn* lay in synthesis, in bringing together the experiences, ideas, and even people, she had been drawn to. Freud regarded this universalizing tendency with suspicion, and he gently contrasted Lou's need for synthesis with his own tendency to chaos. "Even the assurance most clearly expressed in Grabbe's [*Hannibal*] that 'we shall not fall out of this world' doesn't seem sufficient substitute for the surrender of the boundaries of the ego, which can be painful enough." Unified theories (*Weltanschauungen*) are undesirable because they blur the hard-won boundary between the self and the world; Freud's sentiment toward Lou's all-encompassing theories is nearly identical to that with which he greeted the "oceanic feeling" of which he would write years later in *Civilization and Its Discontents*.

Freud contrasted his attitude with Lou's but did not criticize hers; as with the oceanic feeling, and Grabbe's belief in immortality, Freud admired the unifying impulse, even as he felt skeptical of it. Lou's ideas, like those of Rolland and Grabbe, seem to have represented for him another way, closed off to him, of experiencing and understanding the world—erroneous and misleading, perhaps, but also compellingly beautiful.

In her letters to Anna, Lou signaled her agreement with Freud's idea that one enjoyed life in the moment, *because* it was transient. She also apparently embraced Rilke's vision, in the Elegies, of "Things, which live by perishing," a vision in which death is regarded not as a threat but as an essential transformation of existence. Lou tried to harmonize the beliefs of these two men who meant so much to her, and each of whose views she admired and embraced, despite the seemingly irresolvable discord between them. In her hopeful vision, at least, she was able to bring the two perspectives together, perhaps forging in herself the lasting bond that could not be forged between them.

The ardently secular Freud would likely never have accepted Lou's idea of death as a "boundary" to another existence. But perhaps, in light of his notion of the drive toward death as an essential process in universal organic functioning, he might have found common ground with Rilke, at least as far as his scientific skepticism would allow him. Perhaps, despite their differences, in Lou's view of the transience of life, of death and what lay beyond it, Freud and Rilke might have discovered they were not so far apart after all.

7

On September 26, 1939, as the first air-raid sirens began their caterwauling, London gathered to pay its last respects to a late arrival it had made its own. The memorial service for Sigmund Freud at Golders Green was crowded with the devoted, the famous, and the curious. Representatives of the Royal Society, the national academy of science, of which Freud had only months earlier been made a member (to his great pride, joining Darwin and Newton among the ranks of great scientists), stood beside his celebrated friends such as Romain Rolland and Princess Marie Bonaparte. Freud's widow and surviving children were there, as were the remaining members of the "Committee" and the new generation of the movement he had founded. Many in attendance that day were fugitives, exiled in terror from their native countries, to which many of them would never return. Standing in the rain, Freud's longtime friend Stefan Zweig delivered the eulogy, while another old friend, his future biographer Ernest Jones, shared his belief that Freud did not "in any way dread death," and that "what in others expresses itself as religious feeling did so in him as a transcendent belief in the value of life and in the value of love. Thus one can say of him that as never man loved life more, so never man feared death less."

In frank disregard for Jewish law, Freud ordered that his body be cremated. Later his remains were deposited by his relatives in a Greek krater from his collection, where they still lie, in the columbarium at Golders Green, not far from his home in London (now a museum). Given to Freud by Princess Marie Bonaparte, the vase was fired in ancient Greece, its black surfaces covered with painted red figures celebrating a festival in honor of the god Dionysus. The tableau of joyful revelers imbibing wine, rendered on the vase with exquisite care and skill, aptly reflects the Freudian enterprise to tame the impulses in the service of culture.

Perhaps Freud's family, in honoring their patriarch, hoped to call to mind a sentiment like that expressed in Keats's "Ode on a Grecian Urn":

> *. . . Cold Pastoral!*
> *When old age shall this generation waste,*
> *Thou shalt remain, in midst of other woe*
> *Than ours, a friend to man, to whom thou say'st,*
> *"Beauty is truth, truth beauty,—that is all*
> *Ye know on earth, and all ye need to know."*

This sentiment—that fragile mortality is the condition for beauty and truth alike—closely resembles the views Freud himself had expressed in "On Transience."

CONCLUSION

I n the summer of 1904, Freud took a trip with his brother Alexander. The pair had planned to go to Corfu, but his brother's business affairs forced them to shorten their itinerary and, almost on a whim, they wound up in Athens. Freud recorded the effect the trip had on him in a beautiful letter written in 1936, when he was eighty, in honor of his friend Romain Rolland. While standing on the Acropolis, Freud had had what he called a disturbing "derealization"—a sense of surprise at the spectacular sight before him, as though it were unreal, as though it did not really exist. Thinking back on this experience, he at first attributed it to his extravagant affection in youth for the classical world, and the terrific anticipation of seeing its monuments firsthand—the places where Socrates had strolled with Plato, where Phidias had carved the incomparable marble friezes on the Parthenon, where Aeschylus and Sophocles invented drama, where democracy was born. Further reflection, however, forced upon him another explanation.

Freud had noted two characteristics of his "derealization" that it seemed to share with similar experiences, such as déjà vu: first, its "aim at repudiating" some piece of unwelcome knowledge; and second, its "dependence on the past, on the ego's store of memories and upon earlier painful memories which have since fallen to repression."

Tracing his experience on the Acropolis back through his memories, the older Freud corrected his earlier understanding. He hadn't doubted the existence of the Acropolis; rather, in consequence of his early poverty and station in life, he had doubted that he would ever be able to see the Acropolis himself. And to these frustrated longings of his schoolboy days was added another, more recent feeling.

Freud's father had been a man of modest education, and Greece and the cultural ambition it represented meant little to him. Now, on the Acropolis, so long the object of his fascination, Freud understood that he had surpassed his father, who had never seen it and could not appreciate it—and he was overcome with guilt.

Ultimately, Freud believed it was this guilt over his achievement (which he thought also to be guilt for his wish to exceed his father) that had expressed itself in his "derealization." Jacob Freud had died some eight years before his sons' trip to Athens, and the intervening years had been the most eventful in Sigmund's life, encompassing his self-analysis, the completion of *The Interpretation of Dreams*, and the birth of the psychoanalytic movement. Yet despite these triumphs, it was Freud's old grief for his father that returned to trouble him that day in Greece.

Freud's experience on the Acropolis still disturbed him in 1936 because it seemed to resemble the "mystical" experiences he had professed himself insensible of in his discussion of the "oceanic feeling" with Romain Rolland several years earlier and in many conversations throughout his life. Though he was "closed to mysticism as to music," Freud's feelings of guilt toward his dead father could shake his sure sense of reality.

What mysticism, music, and the "oceanic feeling" had in common was their basis in "intuition," a lens onto the world very different from the scientific prism through which Freud had been trained to look.

Intuition—the tool of prophet and poet alike—relied on internal, subjective experience in order to make sense of the world outside. In a letter to Rolland written shortly after the publication of *Civilization and Its Discontents*, Freud contrasted his own attitude toward intuition with that of his friend: "We seem to diverge rather far in the role we assign to intuition. Your mystics rely on it to teach them how to solve the riddle of the universe; we believe that it cannot reveal to us anything but primitive instinctual impulses and attitudes— highly valuable for an embryology of the soul when correctly interpreted, but worthless for orientation in the alien, external world. . . . I am not an out-and-out skeptic. Of one thing I am absolutely positive: there are certain things we cannot know."

Freud believed that "mystical" feelings, far from the otherworldly origins imputed to them by Rolland, were rooted in the forgotten past: the "oceanic feeling" represented a longing to return to the past; "derealization" was the mind's effort to reject the memory of past painful feelings. Mystical experience was thus for Freud a kind of emotional archaeology that offered a dangerous choice: embrace the past and lose oneself in it (in the "oceanic feeling"), or reject it altogether (in "derealization").

As Freud described them, the mysterious sensations of mystical experience sound much like the normal human responses to the ephemeral, fleeting nature of life, and the grief they summon, that he had described in "On Transience." Discussing the poet's reaction to the doomed beauty around him, Freud had written:

> *The proneness to decay of all that is beautiful and perfect can, as we know, give rise to two different impulses in the mind. The one leads to the aching despondency felt by the young poet, while the other leads to rebellion against the fact asserted. No! it is impossible that all this loveliness of Nature and Art, of the world of our sensations and of the world outside, will really fade away into nothing.*

Freud may have been closed to mysticism, to religion, and even, as he claimed, to the transporting beauty of music. But on the Acropolis, he learned he could not ignore the guilt he felt toward his dead father. He could not escape "the powers of destiny" and the inevitability of life's fleeting nature, but he could not refuse to mourn, either.

If he found phenomena such as music and religious feeling hard to fathom, Freud held profound respect for intuition. In a flattering birthday greeting to his fellow Viennese Arthur Schnitzler in 1922, Freud confessed that he felt the writer to be his doppelgänger, and wondered at his ability to "know through intuition—really from a delicate self-observation—everything that I have discovered in other people by laborious work."

Like Freud, Schnitzler had trained as a physician—a calling from which he was eventually distracted by literature. As Freud saw it, he and his doppelgänger were both men of science, drawn by a shared spirit of inquiry into realms far beyond the reach of clinical medicine. In Teutonic myth, a doppelgänger is an uncanny, even monstrous figure, who evokes unease or wonder—not a twin, but a different self, who typically possesses qualities opposite to or repressed or undeveloped in the self. Freud's characterization of Schnitzler this way suggests his feeling of a kinship between his own "scientific" endeavors and those of the writer. In Schnitzler's piercing vision of human motivation, Freud saw a counterpart to his own psychological work, but one coming from a different source, from creative intuition, akin to the personal angels and devils Rilke had feared would be corrected by analysis. Freud felt a strong connection with Schnitzler, yet despite his admiring letter, and although both men were longtime residents of Vienna, he apparently never met him. As with Rilke, "no lasting bond" could be forged with Schnitzler. As much as he admired the ability of these men to follow the inward-pointing compass of their intuition toward poetic truth, something prevented Freud (and perhaps them as well) from pursuing a connection.

Freud's discovery of the secret, meaningful world of dreams led him to the realm of the unconscious, inhabited by the mute shadows and ghosts of unnamed longings, a world seen only in the crevices and dark places of human life: in slips of the tongue, in the hysterias and obsessions of neurotics, and above all, in dreams. Freud's world of the unconscious was a world out of time, where everything, especially what people most cherished, lived on forever in memory.

The dream that opens the all-important chapter 7 of *The Interpretation of Dreams* belonged to a father grieving for his dead son. Exhausted from keeping vigil over his child's body, the man went to sleep in an adjacent room, leaving the child's corpse in the charge of a doddering watchman. Not long after he drifted off, the father dreamt his son was before him, his body aflame, saying, "Father, can't you see I'm burning?" The distraught man awoke to discover that a candle had fallen over and had indeed set his beloved son's corpse on fire.

Freud explained how the remarkable dream allowed the father, even in sleep, to fulfill the duties of the vigil that he kept over his son, and demonstrated the paradoxical manner in which dream life communicates with reality. He said the dream illustrated the first premise of his theory: "A dream is the fulfillment of a wish." In this case, the boy's father wished to see his son alive once more, and this was accomplished through the vision of his child in the dream. Yet in the dream the son was not as the father remembered him in life: he was burning, reflecting the immediate threat. In fulfilling his wish, the dream allowed the father to postpone his return to the terrible reality of his son's death, and to the fire that threatened to kill him, too; but it did so by clothing the boy in the flames of the present, denying his death while alerting the father to the real, imminent danger.

In a letter he wrote to Wilhelm Fliess while working on *The Interpretation of Dreams,* Freud whimsically referred to the book as his "Egyptian Book of Dreams"—an allusion to the Egyptian Book of the Dead. Though his remark was playful, it contained a vital insight into his work: Freud's dream book is also a book of the dead and of mourning. Throughout its nearly seven hundred pages, one finds repeated again and again dreams that Freud interprets to represent death. There is the dream of the "breakfast ship," which reminded Freud of Etruscan artifacts, and in which he saw his own death represented in that of an imaginary governor. In another, Freud dreams of his father's death, in which he hears the phrase "You are requested to close the eyes." There is even one in which he heard that "the pope had died," which came in San Martino di Castrozza during the summer of 1913. In fact, nearly all the dreams reported in the book are Freud's own. Taken together, they form a portrait of his preoccupation with his own mortality and with the losses he had known in the first half of his life: patients, friends, and especially his father, whose death in 1896 led him into depression—and to the self-analysis that produced psychoanalysis.

Alongside the ghosts and phantoms that haunted them, in dreams of death Freud recognized the whole emotional range of grief: guilt, sorrow, and despair, but also rage, aggression, triumph, and relief. Before the idea of death, he discovered that human nature hewed to the contradictory, deeply ambivalent course that was its essence. In the unconscious, grief was as immortal as the dead it mourned, liable to return in every dream, in every thought. And although Freud formulated these laws of human behavior, even he was not exempt from them.

In March 1928, Freud learned of the death of the daughter of his colleague Ernest Jones. In condolence, Freud offered his sympathy and the hard lessons of his own experience; after the loss of his own daughter Sophie and his grandson, he wrote, he "became tired of life permanently." He then proposed a "distraction" for the grieving Jones. Freud had recently come upon a book by the Englishman J. Thomas Looney, who claimed that the works of Shakespeare were not by Shakespeare at all, but were the efforts of Edward de Vere, Earl of Oxford, a prominent member of the Elizabethan court. Freud asked Jones to join his project of looking at the "Shakespeare problem" from a psychoanalytic perspective.

Responding to Freud, Jones was politely appalled; he told his revered master that he had wished from him something more like sympathy and "great wisdom." Dutifully, though, the grieving man took up the Shakespeare matter, and vigorously disputed the thesis of de Vere's authorship.

In another letter to Jones, Freud tried to account for his strange request: "I know of only two avenues of consolation in such a case. The one is bad, because it devalues life itself, and the other, more effective, is of use only to the elderly, not young people such as you and your poor wife. You can easily guess what the second one is. I therefore wrote what I knew was untimely only to keep in touch with you. Let me continue in this vein, for, as an unbelieving fatalist, I can only sink into a state of resignation when faced with the horror of death." He then renewed his proposal of the "distraction."

Continuing in this exchange, Freud responded to his friend's meditation on his own grief, which Jones described as a second killing of his child. Freud rehearsed again the hard choice of mourning: that "one then has the choice of dying oneself or acknowledging the death of the loved one, which again comes very close to your expression that one kills the person." In agreement with Jones, Freud believed that every act of mourning conceals a betrayal, a kind of killing of the loved person by letting the person go; and that guilt over this "murder" endows mourning with its nearly bottomless agony, and explains why so many refuse, unconsciously, to mourn.

Freud described two avenues of consolation in mourning. The first—the notion that the dead are better off, whether because they are in heaven or nowhere at all—"is bad," because it devalues mortal life. The other is hardly preferable, for there can be no doubt of the "second avenue" of which Freud spoke, useful only to the elderly: it was the comforting knowledge that one would soon join the beloved in death. Neither thought offered much consolation, and as a skeptic, Freud sank into hopeless resignation. In grief the choices were stark: One can either die oneself or, through mourning, "acknowledge the death," and assume with it the guilt of the betrayal that it requires. Before death there is no consolation; there is only mourning.

Freud recognized mourning as not only hard and painful, but a necessity—*ananke*—as necessary as life and death themselves. But its necessity presented a paradox. In mourning, by letting go of the dead, one kills again what one misses most; yet the sense of guilt for this "murder" brings with it a renewal of life, because otherwise, swallowed by grief, the mourner would turn his back on life.

Freud believed this because just as life was paradoxically joined with death, the love we feel for those we have lost is bound to our hatred of the beloved's absence, a hatred we direct with full force at ourselves and the empty seat of love within us. In keeping the dead alive within ourselves, through grief, we also keep the hate and guilt alive, which we now turn on ourselves. Such conflicts are the inevitable progression of grief, and the destiny of the ambivalence Freud believed inherent in all love.

At the conclusion of "On Transience," Freud said that mourning should spontaneously cease one day, freeing the energy it consumed for other pursuits. The living and the dead might arrive at an uneasy truce, merely out of exhaustion or, perhaps, out of the transformation of grief, creating something new in memory of the departed.

Along with his pessimistic thoughts, Freud had offered Jones a distraction from his grief: the irritating problem of Shakespeare's identity, whose resolution lay irretrievably in the past, and over which otherwise reasonable people continue to argue today. As inadequate as it was to the task of overcoming the loss of a child, it was, on its face, a puzzling gesture from a normally noble and caring gentleman and physician. Or was it?

Freud was asked in his old age what should be the goals of a healthy, vital life. He is reported to have replied, *"Lieben und Arbeiten"*—to love and to work.

Love had earned a clear place in Freud's estimation. He had come to see in its many forms the source of all emotions, behaviors, and actions. It was the inescapable essence of humanity. But Freud also believed that it was the legacy of humanity to turn the tables on the impulses that drive us, to harness them for use rather than to squander them in rash violence as in the past. Rather than throw a spear, one must take anger and wring from it a verbal insult; in place of rape, romance; in place of action, fiction.

Freud believed that every individual struggles with contradictory impulses and harnesses them in the service of truth, calling on the innately human power of the mind to connect past and present, love and hate, guilt and longing, and to put them outside himself, into the world. This is the work Freud called "sublimation," and he believed it the essence of creativity.

To his student Joan Riviere, Freud once commented on his own methods of working: "Write it, write it, put it down in black and white; that's the way to deal with it; you get it out of your system." To give form to the inchoate world of impulse and feeling, to give it meaning—*Sinn*—one transformed the agonies of the internal world into work, and in doing so put the ghosts to rest.

In the book he was working on at the time of his death, Freud hinted at the meaning the Shakespeare question held for him. In a brief analysis of *Hamlet* as an illustration of the Oedipal drama, he wrote in a footnote that "the name 'William Shakespeare' is most probably a pseudonym behind which there lies concealed a great unknown. Edward de Vere, Earl of Oxford, a man who has been regarded as the author of Shakespeare's works, lost a beloved and admired father while he was still a boy, and completely repudiated his mother, who contracted a new marriage soon after her husband's death."

Freud thought the beauty of *Hamlet* could have been impelled only by a real loss in the life of its author. Like *The Sorrows of Young Werther* for Goethe, *Hamlet* was a work of mourning, a way to exorcise the pain of grief. Long an admirer of Goethe and Shakespeare, Freud looked to them again, for guidance in mourning.

There was no way to avoid the fact of death, but through work, one could express the conflicts it called up within. And not just any work would do, for the "distraction" Freud prescribed for Jones was itself precisely an archaeology of loss. In unraveling the identity of *Hamlet's* author, who, Freud was sure, had created beauty out of grief, Jones might come to bear his own grief more easily. Dispatching him in search of Shakespeare, Freud indicated to his friend that mourning is a vital memorial work, the acknowledgment of loss made possible only through the creativity of memory. It was a lesson Freud had learned countless times: on the Acropolis, in his youthful heartbreak, above all in his dreams.

And Freud himself had taken up a similar distraction more than a decade earlier, in late 1915, while waiting for word from the front of his sons and colleagues, as the world he had loved in his youth collapsed around him.

Late in the summer of 1913, Sigmund Freud took a stroll, with a poet, young but already famous, and a taciturn friend. What transpired that afternoon, the identities of his two companions, even whether the walk took place at all are ultimately unknowable as facts, beyond Freud's essay, which gives them immortal life. Even the places that may have borne witness to these events are gone or changed. The castle at Duino was ruined in

World War I; it has now been restored and welcomes paying tourists. The cities of Germany, especially Berlin and Munich, were disfigured by the terrible ravages of World War II, and were restored and rebuilt to the tastes of a different era. And in Lavarone, only a plaque at the hotel where Freud and his family spent several holidays remains to commemorate the happy months they spent there.

What remains of these moments is a "construction," an interpretative history, like those Freud used in the analysis of his patients' dreams, and his own. Like dream interpretations, such a construction is neither entirely real nor imagined, but like the mycelia linking one mushroom to the next beneath the soil, it weaves Freud's moving recollection together with the names of Rilke, Andreas-Salomé, Jones, Jung, Lincoln, Schnitzler, Rolland, Homer, Plato, Grabbe, Goethe, Schiller, and Shakespeare, and the memories and works in which they live on. This construction joins them all to the world that engendered them, to the Europe of the last century, a world that was already disappearing even as Freud wrote his little essay. It is, in fact, very much like the way in which Freud believed our minds hang on to memories, working them over, joining them to other experiences, and from them fashioning the unique, subjective sense of the world that forms the core of our self or soul or "ego"—our identity.

Despite monuments, the past remains as inaccessible past. The scars and marks of history that they wear do not plead their stories to each new generation who visit, touch, photograph, and consume them. The contours of the past cannot be retraced without the guidance of the emotions and motives that brought a particular history into being. For such guidance, we must turn to the works of artists and storytellers, for only they can make sense of existence by giving names to its themes, to its primal melodies—love and the loss of love; nature and the nature of fate; work and the work of mourning; and the necessity of storytelling. And among these artists and storytellers, we must number the author of "On Transience."

For what Freud did was to rewrite the events of that afternoon, returning to them as one does to a painful memory, and re-create it in accordance with his own longing and desire. In the poet, perhaps Freud caught an image of a part of himself he had lost, saw the poet whom his young passions impelled him to be and dour Ananke, the goddess of necessity, kept him from becoming. Perhaps he felt again in his blood what love does to the instincts, and what freedom is like in a world bounded by social responsibility and moral obligation; knew, finally, the savagery of youth, which is abandoned as the chrysalis of inexperience falls away before maturity.

Seeing himself again in the looking glass of his youth, in the reflection of possibilities lost and time gone forever, Freud was also reminded of death, the theme to which he returned over and over as those he loved passed away and his own body failed. The winter will be replaced by spring, but for each of us the seasons will one day end their pavane. The poet's elegy for transient existence became urgent in the mind of the scientist and reminded him, in light of all he had known and lost, to learn again to mourn. Death—the death of nature within us, and the death of our own possibilities as we traverse the arc of our existence—marks the boundary of life. We strain to see beyond its horizon, to comprehend with our senses what follows, but it is imagination that redeems us, that allows us to create within ourselves a world not bounded by time or death. This is the lesson of mourning, found in the secret history of Freud's fictional walk with a young poet and a taciturn companion.

Like Freud, all individuals tailor their lives according to the themes they find most compelling, and in its setting amid the summer landscape, the conversation of "On Transience" is emblematic of the journey all of us take, from experience to imagination, from mourning to acceptance. This sort of fictional remembering, in life as in literature, is necessary in order to make sense of existence. The universal habit of fashioning stories about the world as one wishes it to be is an expression of the very process Freud outlines in his essay. Through mourning and the triumph of human creativity over loss, the mourner finds again what has been lost within himself. In learning to give himself over to the symphony of life and death, he rediscovers himself, and so realizes the potential inherent in all beings to love and work.

APPENDIX: ON TRANSIENCE

BY SIGMUND FREUD

Translation by James Strachey

Not long ago I went on a summer walk through a smiling countryside in the company of a taciturn friend and of a young but already famous poet. The poet admired the beauty of the scene around us but felt no joy in it. He was disturbed by the thought that all this beauty was fated to extinction, that it would vanish when winter came, like all human beauty and all the beauty and splendour that men have created or may create. All that he would otherwise have loved and admired seemed to him to be shorn of its worth by the transience which was its doom.

The proneness to decay of all that is beautiful and perfect can, as we know, give rise to two different impulses in the mind. The one leads to the aching despondency felt by the young poet, while the other leads to rebellion against the fact asserted. No! it is impossible that all this loveliness of Nature and Art, of the world of our sensations and of the world outside, will really fade away into nothing. It would be too senseless and too presumptuous to believe it. Somehow or other this loveliness must be able to persist and to escape all the powers of destruction.

But this demand for immortality is a product of our wishes too unmistakable to lay claim to reality: what is painful may none the less be true. I could not see my way to dispute the transience of all things, nor could I insist upon an exception in favour of what is beautiful and perfect. But I did dispute the pessimistic poet's view that the transience of what is beautiful involves any loss in its worth.

On the contrary, an increase! Transience value is scarcity value in time. Limitation in the possibility of an enjoyment raises the value of the enjoyment. It was incomprehensible, I declared, that the thought of the transience of beauty should interfere with our joy in it. As regards the beauty of Nature, each time it is destroyed by winter it comes again next year, so that in relation to the length of our lives it can in fact be regarded as eternal. The beauty of the human form and face vanish for ever in the course of our own lives, but their evanescence only lends them a fresh charm. A flower that blossoms only for a single night does not seem to us on that account less lovely. Nor can I understand any better why the beauty and perfection of a work of art or of an intellectual achievement should lose its worth because of its temporal limitation. A time may indeed come when the pictures and statues which we admire to-day will crumble to dust, or a race of men may follow us who no longer understand the works of our poets and thinkers, or a geological epoch may even arrive when all animate life upon the earth ceases; but since the value of all this beauty and perfection is determined only by its significance for our own emotional lives, it has no need to survive us and is therefore independent of absolute duration.

These considerations appeared to me incontestable; but I noticed that I had made no impression either upon the poet or upon my friend. My failure led me to infer that some powerful emotional factor was at work which was disturbing their judgement, and I believed later that I had discovered what it was. What spoilt their enjoyment of beauty must have been a revolt in their minds against mourning. The idea that all this beauty was transient was giving these two sensitive minds a foretaste of mourning over its decease; and, since the mind instinctively recoils from anything that is painful, they felt their enjoyment of beauty interfered with by thoughts of its transience.

Mourning over the loss of something that we have loved or admired seems so natural to the layman that he regards it as self-evident. But to psychologists mourning is a great riddle, one of those phenomena which cannot themselves be explained but to which other obscurities can be traced back. We possess, as it seems, a certain amount of capacity for love—what we call libido—which in the earliest stages of development is directed towards our own ego. Later, though still at a very early time, this libido is diverted from the ego on to objects, which are thus in a sense taken into our ego. If the objects are destroyed or if they are lost to us, our capacity for love (our libido) is once more liberated; and it can then either take other objects instead or can temporarily return to the ego. But why it is that this detachment of libido from its objects should be such a painful process is a mystery to us and we have not hitherto been able to frame any hypothesis to account for it. We only see that libido clings to its objects and will not renounce those that are lost even when a substitute lies ready to hand. Such then is mourning.

My conversation with the poet took place in the summer before the war. A year later the war broke out and robbed the world of its beauties. It destroyed not only the beauty of the countrysides through which it passed and the works of art which it met with on its path but it also shattered our pride in the achievements of our civilization, our admiration for many philosophers and artists and our hopes of a final triumph over the differences between nations and races. It tarnished the lofty impartiality of our science, it revealed our instincts in all their nakedness and let loose the evil spirits within us which we thought had been tamed for ever by centuries of continuous education by the noblest minds. It made our country small again and made the rest of the world far remote. It robbed us of very much that we had loved, and showed us how ephemeral were many things that we had regarded as changeless.

We cannot be surprised that our libido, thus bereft of so many of its objects, has clung with all the greater intensity to what is left to us, that our love of our country, our affection for those nearest us and our pride in what is common to us have suddenly grown stronger. But have those other possessions, which we have now lost, really ceased to have any worth for us because they have proved so perishable and so unresistant? To many of us this seems to be so, but once more wrongly, in my view. I believe that those who think thus, and seem ready to make a permanent renunciation because what was precious has proved not to be lasting, are simply in a state of mourning for what is lost. Mourning, as we know, however painful it may be, comes to a spontaneous end. When it has renounced everything that has been lost, then it has consumed itself, and our libido is once more free (in so far as we are still young and active) to replace the lost objects by fresh ones equally or still more precious. It is to be hoped that the same will be true of the losses caused by this war. When once the mourning is over, it will be found that our high opinion of the riches of civilization has lost nothing from our discovery of their fragility. We shall build up again all that war has destroyed, and perhaps on firmer ground and more lastingly than before.

NOTES

Full citations of works referred to in brief in the notes may be found in the bibliography.

Abbreviations:

AF—Anna Freud
CGJ—Carl Gustav Jung
EJ—Ernest Jones
ES—Eduard Silberstein
FN—Friedrich Nietzsche
LAS—Lou Andreas-Salomé
RMR—Rainer Maria Rilke
SáF—Sándor Ferenczi
SE—The Standard Edition of the Complete Psychological Works of Sigmund Freud, ed. J. Strachey et al.
SF—Sigmund Freud
WF—Wilhelm Fliess

Page 1 "a smiling countryside," and following quotations from Freud's "On Transience": *SE,* vol. 14, pp. 305–307. The complete essay is reprinted, in translation, in the appendix here.

Page 3 The poet with whom Freud: See Lehmann, pp. 423–427 For a dissenting view, see Molnar, *Imagining History.*

Page 5 *"kein ewiger Bund zu flechten":* SF to LAS, July 27, 1916, Pfeiffer, p. 51. It is translated there as "no lasting alliance can be forged"; I have modified that translation, "bond" instead of "alliance."

Page 5 among Freud and Lou and Rilke: Here and throughout this book, I refer to Lou Andreas-Salomé by her first name, despite the obvious gender inequity this supports. I have done so partly for euphony, partly for convenience, and partly out of convention, to maintain the book's emphasis on the relationships among its inhabitants. Rilke, Freud, and Anna Freud all referred to Andreas-Salomé this way (though the impeccably proper Freud would call her "Frau Andreas" until 1922). Andreas-Salomé, in turn, called Anna Freud and Rilke by their first names, and she referred to Freud as "Professor" throughout their friendship. Rilke and Freud referred to each other, and conventionally to themselves, only by surname.

She was, of course, Lou(ise) von Salomé (or Lou Salomé) until her marriage, and in most correspondence afterward referred to herself by her married name. In her literary works and her psychoanalytic writings, she was Lou Andreas-Salomé, and that is how history should remember her.

Page 9 he was fighting for a good cause: SF to Martin Freud, August 26, 1914, cited in M. Freud, p. 180.

Page 9 "I have no doubt": SF to LAS, November 25, 1914, Pfeiffer, p. 21.

Page 12 Yet the accounts that preserve: For varying versions of the visit, see Freedman, pp. 113–115.

Page 13 "If God exists": Rilke, *Samtliche Werke,* vol. 6, p. 967.

Page 13 In a second draft, and following quotations from it: Ibid., pp. 971–978.

Page 13 retelling of the story of the Prodigal Son: See the conclusion of *The Notebooks of Malte Laurids Brigge.*

Page 14 In a later memoir, Lou recalled: Andreas-Salomé, *Looking Back,* p. 86.

Page 15 a light-hearted misunderstanding; "evocative": Ibid.

Page 15 "But we, while we are intent": Rilke, *The Selected Poetry of*

Rainer Maria Rilke, p. 169. All quotations from Rilke's poetry are from Stephen Mitchell's translation.

Page 16 The elegy was an expression: See, for example, Lou's description of a summer walk with Rilke, in July 1913, and "a conversation I had with Rainer one summer afternoon in our garden, when, having completed his Malte project [the novel *The Notebooks of Malte Laurids Brigge*], he had decided not to write anything more, but instead to incorporate what would normally be his work into his approach to real life. We had been discussing how the typical lover often bases the strength of his love on illusions, and how the heart's creative power seems to gain in intensity and fertility, the less it appears to be legitimized by its object. Rainer broke out almost in despair: yes, creativity and creative power were eruptions within oneself and, like those lovers, one was manifesting the loftiest work of humanity! But what the artist created pointed toward a Being beyond the personal level, and it was from that realm that the artist drew his creative inspiration. If he were ever to lose that inspiration, into what abyss would he himself fall!" Andreas-Salomé, *Looking Back,* p. 81.

Page 17 "direst" hour; "it was necessary": From LAS's "Last Appeal," cited ibid., pp. 91, 90.

Page 19 "red ink like a child's exercise in school": RMR to LAS, January 24, 1912, cited ibid., p. 326.

Page 20 became "improbable": RMR to LAS, in letter to Prince Alexander von Thurn und Taxis, February 28, 1911, cited in Freedman, p. 312.

Page 20 "charming company": SF to SáF, December 24, 1915, Falzeder and Brabant, p. 99.

Page 21 "First for fourteen days . . . in body": RMR to SF, February 17, 1916, cited in Molnar, "Entre Rilke et Freud."

Page 21 "I was often": RMR to SF, Febuary 17, 1916, cited in E. Freud, L. Freud, and Grubrich-Simitis, p. 215.

Page 21 "Ernst . . . has at last": SF to LAS, March 21, 1916, Pfeiffer, p. 39.

Page 21 "whom I should like to congratulate": SF to LAS, July 27, 1916, ibid., p. 51. I have modified the translation, from " 'no lasting alliance' " to " 'no lasting bond.' "

Page 22 "No, do not misinterpret": LAS to SF, August, 4, 1916, ibid., p. 51.

Page 23 "You are going to women?": F. Nietzsche, *Thus Spoke Zarathustra*, trans. W. Kaufmann (New York: Penguin, 1978), p. 67. The German reads: *"Du gehst zu Frauen? Vergiss die Peitsche nicht!"*

Page 23 Löwengarten episode: Livingstone, p. 39.

Page 24 "lent his features a quite special magic": L. Andreas-Salomé, *Friedrich Nietzsche in seinen Werken* (1890), cited in Binion, pp. 52–53.

Page 25 "definitely [grew]": Paul Rée to FN, cited in Binion, p. 87.

Page 26 "If I do not hit": FN to Franz Overbeck, cited ibid., p. 100.

Page 27 "And if it is certainly not": FN to Heinrich von Stein, October 15, 1885, cited in Livingstone, p. 54.

Page 28 she would write eight novels: Livingstone, p. 204.

Page 29 a letter from Carl Gustav Jung; "Frau Lou" was invited: CGJ to SF, January 2, 1912, McGuire, p. 478.

Page 30 "He who wants to be original": Sterba, *Reminiscences of a Viennese Psychoanalyst*, p. 120.

Page 31 "She is a highly significant woman": SF to SáF, March 20, 1913, Brabant, Falzeder, and Giampieri-Deutsch, p. 476.

Page 31 "I would like to have got up": LAS to SF, June 30, 1916, Pfeiffer, p. 47.

Page 34 "The finding of an object": S. Freud, *Three Essays on the Theory of Sexuality*, *SE*, vol. 7, p. 222.

Page 35 "Limitation of narcissism": S. Freud, "Group Psychology and the Analysis of the Ego," *SE*, vol. 18, p. 102.

Page 36 "Many a time have I wished": *Symposium* (B. Jowett translation), as quoted in S. Freud, "Notes upon a Case of Obsessional Neurosis," *SE*, vol. 10, p. 240.

Page 36 Aristophanes' account of love: S. Freud, *Beyond the Pleasure Principle*, *SE*, vol. 18, pp. 57–58.

Page 37 "death-drive": Ibid. In his translation of *Beyond the Pleasure Principle*, Strachey renders *Todestrieb* as "death instinct": other translations prefer "death-drive" as closer to the original, and to distinguish it from *Instinkt*, another term Freud often used.

Page 38 In an early draft of "Mourning and Melancholia": See Falzeder and Brabant, pp. 47–48.

Page 38 "The shadow of the object": S. Freud, "Mourning and Melancholia," *SE,* vol. 14, p. 249.

Page 39 "hallucinatory wish psychosis": Falzeder and Brabant, p. 47.

Page 40 In his memoirs, Jung . . . "would risk my authority": Jung, p. 158.

Page 41 But as he recounted later: Ibid., pp. 40–41.

Page 41 While Jung, an advocate: See Jones, vol. 3, p. 384; also SF to CGJ, April 16, 1909, McGuire, pp. 218–220.

Page 42 "My credulity, or at least my willingness": SF to CGJ, April 16, 1909, ibid.

Page 42 "one sees Helen [of Troy]": Ibid., p. 220.

Page 43 *"Es muss süss sein zu sterben":* Jones, vol. 1, p. 317.

Page 43 "How sweet to die": Lines from *Antigone* as cited in P. Weissman, "Antigone—A Pre-Oedipal Old Maid," *Journal of the Hillside Hospital,* 13 (1964), pp. 33–42.

Page 44 "The truth is that these people": S. Freud, "On the History of the Psycho-analytic Movement," *SE,* vol. 14, p. 62.

Page 44 "I have always required"; "My warm friendships": S. Freud, *The Interpretation of Dreams, SE,* vol. 5, p. 483. The phrase "long since have appeared . . ." alludes to the dedication of Goethe's *Faust: "früh sich einst dem trüben Blick gezeigt."*

Page 46 "I was delighted to bring Rainer": Andreas-Salomé, *Freud Journal of Lou Andreas-Salomé,* September 7–8, 1913, p. 169.

Page 47 "unique character resides": Baedeker, p. 490.

Page 47 air "like Champagne": A. Schnitzler, "Fräulein Else" (1924), in *Meistererzählungen* (Frankfurt: S. Fischer, 1969), pp. 473–526.

Page 48 "a place for air cures": Baedeker, p. 460.

Page 48 "an alpine hospice, founded in the twelfth century": Ibid., pp. 454–455.

Page 48 his son Martin later remembered: M. Freud, pp. 134–135.

Page 49 "nothing was worth remembering": S. Freud, "Screen Memories," *SE,* vol. 3, p. 312.

Page 49 "But I am suffering": SF to WF, March 11, 1900, Masson, p. 403; see also M. Freud, p. 47.

Page 49 "I still greatly loved the prison": SF to Max Eitingon, June 6, 1938, E. L. Freud, *Letters of Sigmund Freud, 1873–1939,* pp. 388–389; also cited in Schur, p. 446.

Page 50 "When they went collecting": L. Andreas-Salomé, *Lebensrück-bild,* cited in Peters, p. 26.

Page 52 "splendid isolation": S. Freud, "On the History of the Psycho-analytic Movement," *SE,* vol. 14, p. 22.

Page 52 "One finds oneself suddenly old": S. Freud, "Thoughts for the Times on War and Death," *SE,* vol. 14.

Page 53 "When I was six" . . . "My astonishment": S. Freud, *The Inter-pretation of Dreams, SE,* vol. 4, pp. 205, 206.

Page 53 The mistake: Freud's slip is noted in Naiman, pp. 21–22.

Page 54 "to drink a punch"; "Here and there": SF to WF, September 6, 1897, Masson, p. 263.

Page 55 "It will be so invigorating": SF to WF, December 12, 1897, ibid., p. 286.

Page 55 "If I may use a simile": S. Freud, *The Interpretation of Dreams, SE,* vol. 5, p. 553.

Page 59 "a gifted poet but not successful": M. Freud, p. 111.

Page 60 "a little too sentimental": Ibid.

Page 62 One of his sisters: Ruitenbeck, pp. 143–144.

Page 62 Martin Freud recalled an evening: M. Freud, pp. 37–38.

Page 66 "it seems to me": S. Freud, "Screen Memories," *SE,* vol. 3, p. 312.

Page 66 "Iguanodon, the rapscallion": Scheffel's poem is reprinted in translation in Boehlich, p. 196.

Page 67 "The affection appeared to me": SF to ES, September 4, 1872, ibid., p. 16.

Page 67 "Gisela's beauty is wild" . . . "I have soothed": Ibid., pp. 16–18.

Page 68 "You can imagine that only": SF to ES, October 1, 1875, ibid., p. 133.

Page 69 "Sing me, oh Muse," and following quotations from poem: Ibid., pp. 133–138.

Page 70 "for the moment": Ibid., p. 137.

Page 70   an earlier draft of Freud's epithalamium, and following quotations: Boehlich, p. 188.

Page 72   "Herewith the Formation": Ibid., p. 138.

Page 73   "While producing it": SF to WF, May 25, 1899, Masson, p. 351.

Page 73   "a thirty-eight-year-old man"; "I see a rectangular": S. Freud, "Screen Memories," *SE,* vol. 3, pp. 309, 311.

Page 74   "Those holidays, when I was seventeen," and following quotations: Ibid., pp. 313–315.

Page 81   compiled by the author himself: SF to ES, February 21, 1875, Boehlich, p. 90.

Page 82   "In only a single field": S. Freud, *Totem and Taboo, SE,* vol. 13, p. 90.

Page 83   "in the most condensed fashion": SF to Martha Bernays, July 26, 1883, cited in Jones, vol. 1, p. 175.

Page 84   "Psycho-analysis . . . can thus," and following quotations from the address: S. Freud, "The Goethe Prize," *SE,* vol. 21, pp. 207–212.

Page 84   "a personality of established achievement": introduction to the address, *SE,* vol. 21, p. 206.

Page 87   "know through intuition": SF to Arthur Schnitzler, May 14, 1922, E. L. Freud, *Letters of Sigmund Freud, 1873–1939,* pp. 339–340.

Page 87   "She [Nature] brings forth," and following quotations from essay: "Nature" [A Fragment by Georg Christoph Tobler], in Goethe, *Scientific Studies,* pp. 3–5.

Page 88   In a letter written to his friend; "silently represents": RMR to Sidonie von Nádherný, September 15, 1913, Rilke, *Briefe an Sidonie Nádhernývon Borutin,* p. 195.

Page 88   same apocryphal essay: The essay had been reissued in 1913 by Rilke's publisher, accompanied by a similarly themed work by Ralph Waldo Emerson. Ibid.

Page 89   receiving the prize had made him feel, and following quotations from the address: S. Freud, "The Goethe Prize," *SE,* vol. 21, pp. 208, 211, 212.

Page 90   he cites *Hamlet*: See Jones, vol. 3, p. 381.

Page 91   "the poet [who] confronted": SF to CGJ, April 16, 1909, McGuire, pp. 218–220.

Page 93 essay analyzing Goethe's first memory: "A Childhood Recollection from *Dichtung und Wahrheit*," *SE*, vol. 17, pp. 145–156.

Page 93 the child's wish for his new brother's removal: Ibid., pp. 152–153, 156.

Page 94 "if a man has been his mother's": Ibid., p. 156.

Page 94 "Thus the 'childhood memories'": S. Freud, *The Psychopathology of Everyday Life, SE*, vol. 6, p. 48.

Page 99 "*Alles Vergängliche*": Goethe, *Faust,* p. 502 (Kaufmann's translation modified). *Gleichnis* can mean "image," "symbol," or "likeness."

Page 104 "Hysterics suffer mainly": S. Freud, *Studies on Hysteria, SE,* vol. 2, p. 7.

Page 104 "talking cure": Anna O. was a patient of Josef Breuer's; see Ellenberger, p. 268.

Page 104 "Act as though": S. Freud, "On Beginning the Treatment," *SE,* vol. 12, pp. 134–135.

Page 106 Throughout his working life: Contemporary scientists continue to seek empirical confirmation for Freud's ideas among the rich new insights afforded by neuroscience; see, for instance, Mark Solms, *The Neuropsychology of Dreams* (Mahwah, NJ: Lawrence Erlbaum Associates, 1997).

Page 107 "the lack of good cheer": SF to LAS, November 9, 1915, Pfeiffer, p. 35.

Page 107 "primal father": In a letter to Lou, Freud endorsed in his scheme an epoch of matriarchy, "in the period after the fall of the primal father." SF to LAS, September 2, 1919, ibid., p. 90.

Page 108 "phylogenetic fantasy": See S. Freud, *A Phylogenetic Fantasy: Overview of the Transference Neuroses.*

Page 109 "germ-plasm": S. Freud, "Instincts and Their Vicissitudes," *SE*, vol. 14, p. 125.

Page 111 "anatomy is destiny": S. Freud, "The Dissolution of the Oedipus Complex, *SE*, vol. 19, p. 178.

Page 111 "Witch Phylogenesis": SF to LAS, May 29, 1918, Pfeiffer, p. 80.

Page 111 "Don't we now know": SF to SáF, January 6, 1916, Falzeder and Brabant, p. 101.

Page 113 "A body without much of a soul": Rilke to Viktor von Gebsattel, January 14, 1912, cited in Freedman, p. 326.

Page 114 "It seemed that from": Princess Marie von Thurn und Taxis, *Erinnerungen an Rainer Maria Rilke,* p. 40, cited in Rilke, *The Selected Poetry of Rainer Maria Rilke,* p. 315.

Page 115 In the last days of 1911, and following exchange: RMR to LAS, December 28, 1911, and January 24, 1912; LAS to RMR (telegram), January 22, 1912; all cited in Freedman, p. 326.

Page 116 "red ink"; "drive out": RMR to LAS, January 24, 1912, cited in Freedman, p. 326.

Page 117 "the pleasurable element in artistic activity": LAS to SF, January 30, 1919, Pfeiffer, p. 89.

Page 117 In 1904, Rilke had been horrified: See Freedman, p. 212.

Page 118 "torso is still suffused": Rilke, "Archaic Torso of Apollo," *The Selected Poetry of Rainer Maria Rilke,* p. 61.

Page 119 ". . . How we squander": Rilke, Tenth Duino Elegy, ibid., p. 205.

Page 120 "improbable" to himself: RMR to LAS, in letter to Prince Alexander von Thurn und Taxis, February 28, 1911, cited in Freedman, p. 312.

Page 121 "I was often on the point": RMR to SF, February 17, 1916, cited in E. Freud, L. Freud, and Grubrich-Simitis, p. 215.

Page 122 "People say: 'This Freud'": Sterba, *Reminiscences of a Viennese Psychoanalyst,* p. 119.

Page 122 He told colleagues: Ibid.

Page 124 "Before the problem": S. Freud, "Dostoevsky and Parricide," *SE,* vol. 21, p. 177.

Page 124 Freud was fond of remarking: See his "On the Psychical Mechanism of Hysterical Phenomena: A Lecture," *SE,* vol. 3, pp. 27–39.

Page 126 "It is my hope": SF to WF, August 18, 1897, Masson, p. 262.

Page 127 "I have often observed": S. Freud, "The Moses of Michelangelo," *SE,* vol. 13, pp. 211–213.

Page 128 In October of that year, and following quotations: SF to WF, October 3, 1897, Masson, pp. 268–270.

Page 129 "[This sensation] consists": S. Freud, *Civilization and Its Discontents, SE,* vol. 21, pp. 64–67.

Page 130 "The ego detaches itself": Ibid., p. 68.

Page 131 an imaginary Rome, "in which nothing": Ibid., p. 70.

Page 131 infant's oceanic feeling: The earliest phase of infantile development evoked by the "oceanic feeling" would be a focus of psychoanalysis after Freud, especially in the work of Melanie Klein and D. W. Winnicott. The concept of sublimation in relation to early development is beautifully and vitally explored in Hans Loewald's 1988 monograph *Sublimation;* see also Winnicott's essay "The Use of an Object."

Page 132 "I am closed to mysticism": SF to Romain Rolland, July 20, 1929, E. L. Freud, *Letters of Sigmund Freud, 1873–1939,* pp. 388–389.

Page 134 "If I have understood": S. Freud, *Civilization and Its Discontents, SE,* vol. 21, p. 65. The line from *Hannibal* (translated) is actually "We shall not fall out of this world," as Freud quoted correctly elsewhere.

Page 135 "godless Jew": Cited in Meng and Freud, p. 63.

Page 136 Creativity, Rilke suggested: RMR to LAS, September 10, 1921, Rilke, *Rainer Maria Rilke–Lou Andreas-Salomé Briefwechsel,* pp. 36–38.

Page 136 Lou responded: LAS to RMR, September 22, 1921, ibid., pp. 38–40; also cited in Freedman, p. 476.

Page 140 The images depicted: See Balthus, *Mitsou.*

Page 141 "Now I know myself again": RMR to LAS, February 11, 1922, cited in Freedman, p. 493.

Page 141 "It is one thing to sing," and following quotations from Third Duino Elegy: Rilke, *The Selected Poetry of Rainer Maria Rilke,* pp. 163–165.

Page 142 ". . . why then have to be human," and following quotations from Ninth Duino Elegy: Ibid., pp. 199–201.

Page 143 Tenth Duino Elegy: Ibid., p. 205.

Page 144 "his hero Rilke"; "But not at our house": SF to LAS, March 21, 1916, Pfeiffer, p. 39.

Page 144   "made it quite clear": SF to LAS, July 27, 1916, ibid., p. 51.

Page 144   Freud borrowed . . . "The Song of the Bell": Schiller elided the second word: *"kein ew'ger Bund."* All passages of the poem in English are from Thomas J. Arnold's nineteenth-century translation, found in Retzsch, appendix. I have modified Arnold's rendering of *"kein ew'ger Bund zu flechten"*—"may forged be" rather than "may woven be."

Page 146   "the best of what you know": *"Das Beste was Du weisst, darfst / Du den Buben doch nicht sagen,"* from *Faust,* Part I, scene 4, as quoted in Freud's Goethe Prize address, *SE,* vol. 21, p. 212; see also *The Interpretation of Dreams, SE,* vol. 4, p. 142, and vol. 5, p. 453; and FS to WF, December 3, 1897, and February 9, 1898, in Masson.

Page 146   "a particularly fine example": Minutes of the Vienna Psychoanalytical Society, January 13, 1909, p. 103.

Page 146   "Behind him, a shadowy": Epilogue to "The Song of the Bell," as cited in Anzieu, p. 416.

Page 147   "No, do not misinterpret": LAS to SF, August 4, 1916, Pfeiffer, p. 51.

Page 148   "[Rilke], whom I should like to congratulate": SF to LAS, July 27, 1916, ibid., p. 51.

Page 148   "Although you definitely disclaim": LAS to SF, August 4, 1916, ibid., p. 52.

Page 149   "What the human beast needs": SF to LAS, February 17, 1918, ibid., p. 75.

Page 151   "Christoph Detlev's death": Rilke, *The Notebooks of Malte Laurids Brigge,* p. 21.

Page 152   "Murderers are easy": Fourth Duino Elegy, Rilke, *The Selected Poetry of Rainer Maria Rilke,* p. 173.

Page 153   "René is a no-good": Cited in Freedman, p. 10. Rilke placed a similar scene in *The Notebooks of Malte Laurids Brigge.*

Page 155   "banished and excommunicated": RMR to "L.F.," November 8, 1915, Rilke, *Selected Letters: 1902–1926,* pp. 263–268.

Page 156   He wrote Lou . . . excessive *Onanie:* RMR to LAS, December 8, 1925, ibid., p. 475. See also LAS to RMR, December 12, 1925, ibid., pp. 479–482.

Page 157 "I don't know how many hells": RMR to LAS, December 13, 1926, cited in Freedman, p. 549.

Page 158 "Rose, pure contradiction, joy": Rilke's epitaph, as translated ibid., p. 550. The German reads: "*Rose, oh reiner Widerspruch, Lust / Niemandes Schlaf zu sein unter soviel Lidern.*"

Page 159 "With me crabbed age": SF to LAS, May 11, 1927, Pfeiffer, p. 165.

Page 160 "eruptions" of youth, and following quotations: May 20, 1927, ibid., pp. 165–168.

Page 162 "the great poet": S. Freud, "Lou Andreas-Salomé," *SE*, vol. 23, pp. 297–298.

Page 163 puzzling dream, and following quotations: S. Freud, *The Interpretation of Dreams, SE*, vol. 5, pp. 463–464.

Page 165 In February 1923: For a definitive account of Freud's last illness, see Schur.

Page 165 "I detected two months ago": SF to EJ, April 25, 1923, Paskauskas, p. 521.

Page 166 "a painful swelling": SF to SáF, November 6, 1917, Falzeder and Brabant, p. 245.

Page 167 "I am not obeying": SF to WF, November 27, 1893, Masson, p. 61.

Page 167 In the letters he wrote: See Schur.

Page 168 When told that he would require, and Holzknecht exchange: Sterba, *Reminiscences of a Viennese Psychoanalyst*, pp. 104–105.

Page 168 "You are to be admired," and following exchange: Schur, p. 427.

Page 169 While he and Freud were walking; "that I might": S. Freud, "An Autobiographical Study," *SE*, vol. 20, p. 52.

Page 169 "I am still walking": SF to Marie Bonaparte, April 26, 1927, cited in Schur, pp. 391–392.

Page 170 "What an amount of good naturedness": SF to LAS, May 16, 1935, Pfeiffer, pp. 208–209.

Page 170 "Immortality evidently": SF to Marie Bonaparte, August 13, 1937, E. L. Freud, *Letters of Sigmund Freud, 1879–1937*, p. 436.

Page 171 "oceans of time": S. Freud, "Some Psychical Consequences of the Anatomical Distinction Between the Sexes," *SE,* vol. 19, p. 248.

Page 171 On April 9, 1938, Freud noted: Molnar, *The Diary of Sigmund Freud 1929–1939,* p. 233.

Page 172 "I think that if the chow": H.D. [Hilda Doolittle] to Winifred Bryher, March 1, 1933, cited in Tolpin, p. 33.

Page 172 Jo-Fie, Yu, Lun: The spelling of the names of Freud's dogs, and their order of succession, are given variously in various sources.

Page 173 "He admired them": A. Freud, introduction to Bonaparte, *Topsy* (1994).

Page 174 In the course of her analysis: This anecdote appears in Bonaparte, *Chronos, Eros, Thanatos,* pp. 67–70.

Page 175 "case" of Alcibiades: S. Freud, "Notes upon a Case of Obsessional Neurosis," *SE,* vol. 10, p. 240.

Page 176 "In this way," and following quotations: Bonaparte, *Topsy* (1940), pp. 70–71.

Page 176 "carnal mortality" ("*mortalité charnelle*"): The passage is on p. 117 of the original French, and on p. 165 of the German translation; see Bonaparte, *Topsy* entries in the bibliography.

Page 177 "That is why Topsy": Bonaparte, *Topsy* (1940), p. 71.

Page 177 "Everything will perish," and following quotations (including Freud's letter): Bonaparte, "Deux penseurs devant l'abîme" [Two Thinkers Before the Abyss], pp. 310–311.

Page 180 "To the Editor of Time and Tide": S. Freud, "Anti-Semitism in England," *SE,* vol. 23, p. 301 (letter dated November 16, 1938).

Page 182 "She is perfect": H.D. [Doolittle], *Tribute to Freud,* pp. 68–69.

Page 182 "a source of extraordinary invigoration": SF to WF, December 6, 1896, Masson, p. 214.

Page 183 "I have sacrificed a great deal": SF to Stefan Zweig, February 7, 1931, cited in Gamwell and Wells, p. 184.

Page 183 "the psychoanalyst, like the archaeologist": Gardiner, p. 139.

Page 183 Freud imagined the mind: S. Freud, *Civilization and Its Discontents, SE,* vol. 21, p. 70.

Page 184 "the priceless though mutilated": S. Freud, *Three Essays on the*

Theory of Sexuality, SE, vol. 7, p. 12; see also "Constructions in Analysis," *SE,* vol. 23, p. 258.

Page 186 "Here are my respondents": SF in conversation with H. R. Lenormand, cited in Ruitenbeck, p. 251.

Page 186 "Forms may pass away": SF to Ernst Simmel, November 11, 1928, E. L. Freud, *Letters of Sigmund Freud, 1873–1939,* pp. 382–383.

Page 187 "Judging by the priority": SF to Rachel Berdach, cited in Schur, p. 528.

Page 187 "the final phase began": Schur, pp. 527–528.

Page 187 "This was the proper book": Ibid., p. 528.

Page 188 "when the time comes": Ibid., p. 408.

Page 188 "Dear Schur, doubtless": Ibid., p. 529.

Page 189 Yet in the early drafts: See Gay, p. 651, and especially note pp. 739–740.

Page 191 "It has had a strange effect": SF to SáF, September 16, 1930, Falzeder, Brabant, and Giampieri-Deutsch, p. 399.

Page 192 In May 1923 . . . Anna Freud . . . wrote Lou Andreas-Salomé: The letters may be found in Rothe and Weber, pp. 186ff.

Page 192 Walking with her father: AF to LAS, May 12, 1923, ibid.

Page 193 Amid these melancholy reflections: AF to LAS, May 24, 1923, ibid. Although Rilke's Elegies would not be published until June 1923, weeks after Anna wrote her letter, she had read the Ninth Elegy with Lou while visiting her in 1922, shortly after Lou received the newborn poems from Rilke. Like her brother Ernst, Anna—at the time an aspiring writer herself—idolized Rilke, and one can imagine her excitement at being able to read the Elegies in the poet's own hand, before others knew of them. In her letter Anna regretted that she had not copied out the elegy for herself; a short while later, Lou sent Anna a copy.

Page 193 ". . . how even lamenting": Rilke, *The Selected Poetry of Rainer Maria Rilke,* p. 201.

Page 194 As she explained . . . Anna believed: AF to LAS, May 24, 1923, Rothe and Weber, pp. 189–191.

Page 194 In response . . . Lou suggested: LAS to AF, May 15, 1923, ibid., pp. 187–189.

Page 195 "'understander' *par excellence*": SF to LAS, May 25, 1916, Pfeiffer, p. 45.

Page 195 "The unity of this world": SF to LAS, July 30, 1915, ibid., p. 32.

Page 196 Lou signaled her agreement: LAS to AF, May 15, 1923, ibid., p. 188.

Page 197 Ernest Jones, shared his belief: Jones, vol. 3, p. 246.

Pages 198 "... Cold Pastoral!": "Ode on a Grecian Urn," J. Keats, *Selected Poetry*, ed. P. de Man (New York: New American Library/Signet, 1966), p. 253.

Page 199 Freud recorded the effect, and following quotations from the letter: S. Freud, "A Disturbance of Memory on the Acropolis," *SE*, vol. 22, pp. 239–248.

Page 201 "closed to mysticism": SF to Romain Rolland, July 20, 1929, E. L. Freud, *Letters of Sigmund Freud, 1873–1939*, pp. 388–389.

Page 201 "We seem to diverge": SF to Romain Rolland, January 19, 1930, ibid., pp. 392–393.

Page 203 In a flattering birthday greeting: SF to Arthur Schnitzler, May 14, 1922, ibid., p. 339.

Page 204 The dream that opens: S. Freud, *The Interpretation of Dreams*, *SE*, vol. 5, p. 509.

Page 205 "A dream is the fulfillment": Ibid., *SE*, vol. 4, p. 121.

Page 205 In a letter ... "Egyptian Book of Dreams": SF to WF, August 6, 1899, Masson, p. 366 (translation modified).

Page 205 "breakfast ship": S. Freud, *The Interpretation of Dreams, SE*, vol. 5, pp. 463–464.

Page 205 "You are requested": Ibid., *SE*, vol. 4, pp. 317–318.

Page 205 "the pope had died": When Freud awoke, he could make no sense of the dream, until his wife remarked on the racket the church bells had made that morning. Freud included this dream in a later edition of *The Interpretation of Dreams* and in two other works to illustrate the influence of the outside world on a sleeper's dreams. His dream, he explained, had taken vengeance on the pious Tyrolese for disturbing his sleep, by killing off their pope. Yet he went on to say that, important as external events may be in giving rise to a particular dream, they cannot go very far to shed light on its deeper meaning.

Macbeth, he offered by way of analogy, was written for a coronation, but this circumstance of its creation did little to explain the power of its language or elucidate its themes.

Freud's dream also may have incorporated the expression *"Habemus papam"* (We have a pope), which he himself had used in 1897, in announcing his "seduction theory" of neurosis, as he sardonically remarked to his friend Wilhelm Fliess. The traditional Latin phrase used to announce the election of a new pope might also be taken to mean "We have a father." Freud intended this meaning as a reference to the frequent role of the father in traumas of seduction.

A new pope is chosen only on the death or abdication of his predecessor. Behind Freud's own interpretation, there is a pathos to his dream; with the impending break from his ostensible successor Jung only weeks away, the pope of whose death he dreamt may well have been himself.

Page 206 In condolence, Freud offered: SF to EJ, March 11, 1928, Paskauskas, p. 643.

Page 207 Responding to Freud, Jones: EJ to SF, April 29 and October 27, 1928, ibid., pp. 644–645 and 650–651.

Page 207 "I know of only two avenues," and following quotations: SF to EJ, May 3 and October 27, 1928, ibid., pp. 646–647 and 652–653.

Page 209 *"Lieben und Arbeiten"*: Erikson, pp. 264–265.

Page 210 "Write it, write it": Riviere, p. 146.

Page 210 "the name 'William Shakespeare'": S. Freud, "An Outline of Psycho-analysis," *SE,* vol. 23, p. 192.

Page 210 Freud believed the beauty: While in his later years Freud was an implacable Oxfordian, he initially (in *The Interpretation of Dreams*), proposed the death of Hamnet, son of the historical William Shakespeare, as the catalyst for *Hamlet.* Intriguingly, although Freud announced his new theory of Shakespeare's identity in a footnote to a 1930 edition of *The Interpretation of Dreams,* he did not alter his original interpretation (see *SE,* vol. 4, pp. 264–266, and Strachey's notes).

Page 211 "On Transience": *SE,* vol. 14, pp. 305–307.

SELECTED BIBLIOGRAPHY

Andreas-Salomé, L. *The Freud Journal of Lou Andreas-Salomé.* Trans. S. A. Leavy. New York: Basic Books, 1964.

Andreas-Salomé, L. *Looking Back: Memoirs.* Ed. E. Pfeiffer. Trans. B. Mitchell. New York: Paragon, 1990.

Anzieu, D. *Freud's Self-Analysis.* Trans. P. Graham. Madison, CT: International Universities Press, 1986.

Baedeker, K. *Handbuch für Reisende: Südbayern, Tirol, Salzburg . . .* Leipzig: Karl Baedeker, 1912.

Balthus [Balthasar Klossowski de Rola]. *Mitsou* (1921). New York: The Metropolitan Museum of Art, 1984.

Berliner Goethesbund. *Das Land Goethes: Ein vaterlandisches Gedenkbuch 1914–1916.* Stuttgart and Berlin: Deutsche Verlags-Anstalt, 1916.

Bernfeld, S. "Freud's Earliest Theories and the School of Helmholtz." *The Psychoanalytic Quarterly,* 13 (1944), pp. 341–362.

Bernfeld, S. "Freud's Studies on Cocaine, 1884–1887." *Journal of the American Psychoanalytic Association,* 1 (1953), pp. 581–613.

Bernfeld, S. "Sigmund Freud, M.D., 1882–1885." *The International Journal of Psychoanalysis,* 32 (1951), pp. 204–217.

Bernfeld, S., et al. "Freud's Early Childhood." *Bulletin of the Menninger Clinic,* 8 (1944), pp. 107–115.

Bernfeld, S., et al. "Freud's First Year in Practice, 1886–1887." *Bulletin of the Menninger Clinic,* 16 (1952), pp. 37–49.

Binion, R. *Frau Lou: Nietzsche's Wayward Disciple.* Princeton, NJ: Princeton University Press, 1968.

Binswanger, L. *Sigmund Freud: Reminiscences of a Friendship.* New York: Grune & Stratton, 1957.

Boehlich, W., ed. *The Letters of Sigmund Freud to Eduard Silberstein: 1871–1881.* Trans. A. J. Pomerans. Cambridge, MA: Belknap Press of Harvard University Press, 1990.

Bonaparte, M. *Chronos, Eros, Thanatos.* London: Imago, 1952.

Bonaparte, M. "Time and the Unconscious." *The International Journal of Psychoanalysis,* 21 (1940), pp. 427–468.

Bonaparte, M. *Topsy, chow-chow au poil d'or.* Paris: Denoël et Steele, 1937.

Bonaparte, M. *Topsy, der goldhaarige Chow.* Trans. A. and S. Freud. Amsterdam: Allert de Lange, 1939.

Bonaparte, M. *Topsy: The Story of a Golden-Haired Chow.* London: Pushkin, 1940.

Bonaparte, M. *Topsy: The Story of a Golden-Haired Chow.* New Brunswick, NJ: Transaction, 1994.

Bonaparte, M. "Deux penseurs devant l'abîme" [Two Thinkers Before the Abyss]. *Revue française de psychanalyse,* no. 3 (July–September 1956), pp. 307–315.

Brabant, E., E. Falzeder, and P. Giampieri-Deutsch, eds. *The Correspondence of Sigmund Freud and Sándor Ferenczi,* vol. 1: *1908–1914.* Trans. P. Hoffer. Cambridge, MA: Belknap Press of Harvard University Press, 1993.

Cheshire, N. M. "The Empire of the Ear: Freud's Problem with Music." *The International Journal of Psychoanalysis,* 77 (1996), pp. 1127–1168.

Davis, F. B. "Three Letters from Sigmund Freud to André Breton." *Journal of the American Psychoanalytic Association,* 21 (1973), pp. 127–134.

Deri, F., and D. Brunswick, trans. "Freud's Letters to Ernst Simmel." *Journal of the American Psychoanalytic Association,* 12 (1964), pp. 93–109.

H.D. [Doolittle, H.]. *Tribute to Freud.* New York: Pantheon, 1956.

Eissler, K. R. "Creativity and Adolescence: The Effect of Trauma in Freud's

Adolescence." *The Psychoanalytic Study of the Child*, 33 (1978), pp. 461–518.

Ellenberger, H. F. "The Story of 'Anna O.': A Critical Review with New Data." In *Beyond the Unconscious*. Princeton, NJ: Princeton University Press, 1993, pp. 254–272.

Erikson, E. *Childhood and Society*. 2nd ed. New York: W. W. Norton, 1963.

Falzeder, E., and E. Brabant, eds. *The Correspondence of Sigmund Freud and Sándor Ferenczi*, vol. 2: *1914–1919*. Trans. P. Hoffer. Cambridge, MA: Belknap Press of Harvard University Press, 1996.

Falzeder, E., and E. Brabant, with P. Giampieri-Deutsch, eds. *The Correspondence of Sigmund Freud and Sándor Ferenczi*, vol. 3: *1920–1933*. Trans. P. Hoffer. Cambridge, MA: Belknap Press of Harvard University Press, 2000.

Flannery, J. G. "Freud's Acropolis Revisited." *International Review of Psychoanalysis*, 7 (1980), pp. 347–352.

Freedman, R. *Life of a Poet: A Biography of Rainer Maria Rilke*. New York: Farrar, Straus & Giroux, 1996.

Freud, E. L., ed. *Letters of Sigmund Freud, 1873–1939*. Trans. T. and J. Stern. London: Hogarth, 1961.

Freud, E. L., ed. *The Letters of Sigmund Freud and Arnold Zweig*. Trans. E. and W. Robson-Scott. New York: Harcourt, Brace & World, 1970.

Freud, E., L. Freud, and I. Grubrich-Simitis, eds. *Sigmund Freud: His Life in Pictures and Words*. Trans. C. Trollope. New York: Harcourt Brace Jovanovich, 1978.

Freud, E. L., and H. Meng, eds. *Sigmund Freud–Oskar Pfister: Briefe, 1909–1939*. Frankfurt: S. Fischer, 1963.

Freud, M. *Glory Reflected*. London: Angus & Robertson, 1957.

Freud, S., and L. Andreas-Salomé. *Sigmund Freud and Lou Andreas-Salomé: Letters*. Ed. E. Pfeiffer. Trans. W. Robson-Scott. New York: W. W. Norton, 1985.

Freud, S., and C. G. Jung. *The Freud/Jung Letters: The Correspondence Between Sigmund Freud and Carl Gustav Jung*. Ed. W. McGuire. Trans. R. Manheim and R. F. C. Hull. London: Hogarth and Kegan Paul, 1974.

Freud, S., and A. Zweig. *The Letters of Sigmund Freud and Arnold Zweig.* Ed. E. L. Freud. New York: New York University Press, 1970.

Gamwell, L., and R. Wells., eds. *Sigmund Freud and Art: His Personal Collection of Antiquities.* London: Freud Museum, 1989.

Gardiner, M. *The Wolf Man.* New York: Basic Books, 1971.

Gay, P. *Freud: A Life for Our Time.* New York: W. W. Norton, 1988.

Ginsburg, L. M., and S. A. Ginsburg. "Paradise in the Life of Sigmund Freud: Imagery and Paradoxes." *International Review of Psychoanalysis,* 19 (1992), pp. 285–308.

Goethe, J. W. von. *Faust.* Trans. W. Kaufmann. Garden City, NY: Anchor, 1962.

Goethe, J. W. von. *Scientific Studies* (vol. 12 of *Goethe: The Collected Works*). Ed. D. Miller. Princeton, NJ: Princeton University Press, 1955.

Harrison, I. B. "Reconsideration: Freud's 'Disturbance of Memory on the Acropolis.'" *Journal of the American Psychoanalytic Association,* 14 (1966), pp. 518–527.

Jones, E. *The Life and Work of Sigmund Freud.* New York: Basic Books, 1957.

Jung, C. G. *Memories, Dreams, Reflections.* New York: Pantheon, 1963.

Lehmann, H. "A Conversation Between Freud and Rilke." *The Psychoanalytic Quarterly,* 35 (1966), pp. 423–427.

Leppmann, W. *Rilke: A Life.* Trans. the author with R. M. Stockman. New York: Fromm, 1984.

Livingstone, A. *Lou Andreas-Salomé.* London: Gordon Fraser, 1984.

Loewald, H. W. *Sublimation: Inquiries into Theoretical Psychoanalysis.* New Haven, CT: Yale University Press, 1988.

Mann, T. *Freud, Goethe, and Wagner.* New York: Alfred A. Knopf, 1937.

Masson, J., ed. and trans. *The Complete Letters of Sigmund Freud to Wilhelm Fliess, 1887–1904.* Cambridge, MA: Belknap Press of Harvard University Press, 1985.

Masson, J. M., and T. C. Masson. "Buried Memories on the Acropolis: Freud's Response to Mysticism and Anti-Semitism." *The International Journal of Psychoanalysis,* 59 (1978), pp. 199–208.

McGuire, W., ed. *The Freud/Jung Letters: The Correspondence Between*

Sigmund Freud and C. G. Jung. Trans. R. Manheim and R. F. C. Hull. Princeton, NJ: Princeton University Press, 1974.

Meisel, P., and W. Kendrick, eds. *Bloomsbury/Freud: The Letters of James and Alix Strachey, 1924–1925.* New York: Basic Books, 1985.

Meng, H., and E. L. Freud, eds. *Psychoanalysis and Faith: Dialogues with the Reverend Oskar Pfister.* Trans. E. Mosbacher. New York: Basic Books, 1963.

Molnar, M., ed. and trans. *The Diary of Sigmund Freud 1929–1939: A Record of the Final Decade.* New York: Charles Scribner's Sons, 1992.

Molnar, M. "Entre Rilke et Freud." In S. Michaud and G. Stieg, eds., *Rilke et son amie Lou Andreas-Salomé.* Paris: Presses de la Sorbonne Nouvelle/Bibliothèque Nationale de France, 2001.

Molnar, M. "Imagining History." Paper delivered at the Freud Museum, London/THERIP conference "Lived Events and Remembered Events in Psychoanalysis," Tavistock Clinic, London, March 15, 2003.

Naiman, J. "Freud, Odysseus, and Middle Age." *Canadian Journal of Psychoanalysis,* 2 (1994), pp. 19–28.

Paskauskas, R. A., ed. *The Complete Correspondence of Sigmund Freud and Ernest Jones, 1908–1939.* Cambridge, MA: Harvard University Press, 1993.

Peters, H. *My Sister, My Spouse: A Biography of Lou Andreas-Salomé.* New York: W. W. Norton, 1962.

Pfeiffer, E., ed. *Sigmund Freud and Lou Andreas-Salomé: Letters.* Trans. W. and E. Robson-Scott. London: Hogarth, 1972.

Pollock, G. H. "On Freud's Psychotherapy of Bruno Walter." *The Annual of Psychoanalysis,* 3 (1975), pp. 287–296.

Retzsch, M. *Umrisse zu Schiller's Lied von der Glocke.* Stuttgart: J. G. Cotta, 1834.

Riviere, J. "A Character Trait of Freud's." In J. D. Sutherland, ed., *Psychoanalysis and Contemporary Thought.* London: Hogarth, 1958, pp. 145–149.

Roazen, P. "Freud's Last Will: Introduction." *Journal of the American Academy of Psychoanalysis,* 18 (1990), pp. 383–391.

Rothe, D. A., and I. Weber, eds. "—*als käm ich heim zu Vater und*

Schwester": *Lou Andreas-Salomé–Anna Freud Briefwechsel 1919–1937.* Göttingen: Wallstein, 2001.

Ruitenbeck, H., ed. *Freud As We Knew Him.* Detroit: Wayne State University Press, 1973.

Schur, M. *Freud: Living and Dying.* New York: International Universities Press, 1972.

Sterba, R. *Erinnerungen eines Wiener Psychoanalytikers.* Frankfurt: S. Fischer, 1985. (English version follows.)

Sterba, R. *Reminiscences of a Viennese Psychoanalyst.* Detroit: Wayne State University Press, 1982.

Strachey, J., et al., eds. *The Standard Edition of the Complete Psychological Works of Sigmund Freud,* 24 vols. London: Hogarth, 1953–1974. (See itemized list of works below.)

Tolpin, M. "'She is perfect . . . only she has lost her spear': The Goddess Athene, Freud, and H.D." *The Annual of Psychoanalysis,* 19 (1991), pp. 33–50.

Trosman, H. "Freud and the Controversy over Shakespearean Authorship." *Journal of the American Psychoanalytic Association,* 13 (1965), pp. 475–498.

Trosman, H. "The Freud Library." *Journal of the American Psychoanalytic Association,* 21 (1973), pp. 646–687.

Werman, D. S. "Sigmund Freud and Romain Rolland." *International Review of Psychoanalysis,* 4 (1977), pp. 225–242.

Werman, D. S. "Stefan Zweig's Relationship to Freud and Rolland: Auxiliary Ego Ideal." *International Review of Psychoanalysis,* 6 (1979), pp. 77–96.

Winnicott, D.W. "The Use of an Object." *The International Journal of Psychoanalysis,* 50 (1969), pp. 711–716.

Wittels, F. *Freud and His Time.* New York: Liveright, 1931.

Yerushalmi, Y. *Freud's Moses: Judaism Terminable and Interminable.* New Haven, CT, and London: Yale University Press, 1991.

Young-Bruehl, E. *Anna Freud: A Biography.* New York: Summit, 1988.

Works by Sigmund Freud

All citations in the notes refer to *The Standard Edition of the Complete*

Psychological Works of Sigmund Freud, 24 vols. Ed. J. Strachey et al. London: Hogarth, 1953–1974.

Studies on Hysteria (1895). *SE,* vol. 2.

"Screen Memories" (1899). *SE,* vol. 3, pp. 301–322.

The Interpretation of Dreams (1899). *SE,* vols. 4–5.

Three Essays on the Theory of Sexuality (1905). *SE,* vol. 7.

"Creative Writers and Day-dreaming" (1908). *SE,* vol. 9, pp. 143–153.

"Family Romances" (1909). *SE,* vol. 9, pp. 235–244.

"Notes upon a Case of Obsessional Neurosis" (1909). *SE,* vol. 10, pp. 155–318.

"Contributions to a Discussion on Masturbation" (1912). *SE,* vol. 12, pp. 243–254.

"The Dynamics of Transference" (1912). *SE,* vol. 12, pp. 99–108.

"Recommendations to Physicians Practising Psycho-analysis" (1912). *SE,* vol. 12, pp. 111–120.

"The Claims of Psycho-analysis to Scientific Interest" (1913). *SE,* vol. 13, pp. 165–190.

"The Occurrence in Dreams of Material from Fairy Tales" (1913). *SE,* vol. 12, pp. 279–288.

"On Beginning the Treatment" (1913). *SE,* vol. 12, pp. 123–144.

"Preface to Bourke's Scatalogic [*sic*] Rites of All Nations." (1913). *SE,* vol. 12, pp. 333–340.

"On Psycho-analysis." (1913). *SE,* vol. 12, pp. 205–212.

"The Theme of the Three Caskets" (1913). *SE,* vol. 12, pp. 291–301.

Totem and Taboo (1913). *SE,* vol. 13, pp. 1–161.

"Two Lies Told by Children" (1913). *SE,* vol. 12, pp. 303–310.

"*Fausse Reconnaissance, 'Déjà Raconte'* in Psycho-analytic Treatment" (1914). *SE,* vol. 13, pp. 201–207.

"The Moses of Michelangelo" (1914). *SE,* vol. 13, pp. 211–238.

"On the History of the Psycho-analytic Movement" (1914). *SE,* vol. 14, pp. 7–66.

"On Narcissism: An Introduction" (1914). *SE,* vol. 14, pp. 73–102.

"Remembering, Repeating, Working-through" (1914). *SE,* vol. 12, pp. 147–156.

"Some Reflections on Schoolboy Psychology" (1914). *SE*, vol. 13, pp. 241–244.

"A Connection Between a Symbol and a Symptom" (1915). *SE*, vol. 14, pp. 339–340.

"A Mythological Parallel to a Visual Obsession" (1915). *SE*, vol. 14, pp. 337–338.

"Repression" (1915). *SE*, vol. 14, pp. 146–158.

"Thoughts for the Times on War and Death" (1915). *SE*, vol. 14, pp. 273–300.

"The Unconscious" (1915). *SE*, vol. 14, pp. 166–204.

Introductory Lectures on Psycho-Analysis (parts 1 and 2) (1916). *SE*, vol. 15, pp. 9–239.

"On Transience" (1916). *SE*, vol. 14, pp. 305–307. (Published in a different translation in *The International Journal of Psychoanalysis*, 23, pp. 84–85.)

"A Childhood Recollection from *Dichtung und Wahrheit*" (1917). *SE*, vol. 17, pp. 145–156.

"Mourning and Melancholia" (1917 [1915]). *SE*, vol. 14, pp. 237–258.

"From the History of an Infantile Neurosis" (1918). *SE*, vol. 17, pp. 7–122.

"Introduction to 'Psycho-analysis and the War Neuroses.'" (1919). *SE*, vol. 17, pp. 207–210.

"The 'Uncanny'" (1919). *SE*, vol. 17, pp. 219–256.

"Victor [*sic*] Tausk" (1919). *SE*, vol. 17, pp. 273–275.

Beyond the Pleasure Principle (1920). *SE*, vol. 18, pp. 7–64.

"Group Psychology and the Analysis of the Ego" (1921). *SE*, vol. 18, pp. 69–143.

"Dreams and Telepathy" (1922). *SE*, vol. 18, pp. 197–220.

"The Ego and the Id" (1923). *SE*, vol. 19, pp. 12–66.

"Some Psychical Consequences of the Anatomical Distinction Between the Sexes" (1925). *SE*, vol. 19, pp. 248–258.

"To Romain Rolland" (1926). *SE*, vol. 20, p. 279.

"The Future of an Illusion" (1927). *SE*, vol. 21, pp. 5–56.

"Dostoevsky and Parricide" (1928). *SE*, vol. 21, pp. 177–196.

"Fetishism" (1928). *SE*, vol. 21, p. 152.

Civilization and Its Discontents (1929). *SE*, vol. 21, pp. 64–145.

"The Goethe Prize" (1930). *SE*, vol. 21, pp. 207–212.

"To Thomas Mann on His Sixtieth Birthday" (1935). *SE*, vol. 22, p. 255.

"A Disturbance of Memory on the Acropolis" (1936). *SE*, vol. 22, pp. 239–248.

"Lou Andreas-Salomé" (1937). *SE*, vol. 23, pp. 297–298.

"Anti-Semitism in England" (1938). *SE*, vol. 23, p. 301.

"A Comment on Anti-Semitism" (1938). *SE*, vol. 23, pp. 291–293.

"Constructions in Analysis" (1938). *SE*, vol. 23, pp. 257–269.

"Moses an Egyptian" (1938). *SE*, vol. 23, p. 7.

"An Outline of Psycho-analysis." (1940 [1938]). *SE*, vol. 23, pp. 144–207.

Freud, S. *A Phylogenetic Fantasy: Overview of the Transference Neuroses.* Ed. I. Grubrich-Simitis. Trans. A. Hoffer and P. Hoffer. Cambridge, MA: Harvard University Press, 1987.

Works by Rainer Maria Rilke

Briefe 1897–1926. Ed. R. Sieber-Rilke and K. Altheim. Frankfurt: Insel, 1975.

Briefe an Sidonie Nádherný von Borutin. Ed. B. Blume. Frankfurt: Insel, 1973.

Diaries of a Young Poet. Trans. E. Snow and M. Winkler. New York: W. W. Norton, 1997.

Duino Elegies and the Sonnets to Orpheus. Trans. A. Poulin. Boston: Houghton Mifflin, 1977.

The Notebooks of Malte Laurids Brigge. Trans M. Herder Norton. New York: W. W. Norton, 1964.

Rainer Maria Rilke–Lou Andreas Salomé Briefwechsel. Ed. E. Pfeiffer. Frankfurt: Insel, 1975.

Samtliche Werke, 6 vols. Ed. E. Zinn. Frankfurt: Insel, 1955–1966.

Selected Letters: 1902–1926. Trans. R. F. C. Hull. London: Quartet, 1988.

The Selected Poetry of Rainer Maria Rilke. Trans. S. Mitchell. New York: Vintage, 1989.

Where Silence Reigns: Selected Prose. Trans. G. C. Houston. New York: New Directions, 1978.